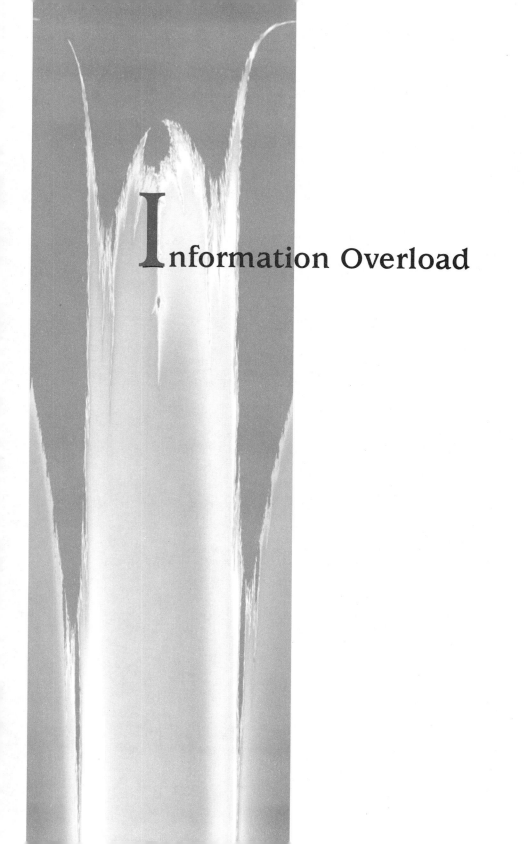

Information Overload

Selected Titles from the
YOURDON PRESS COMPUTING SERIES
Ed Yourdon, *Advisor*

Information Overload

Creating Value with The New Information Systems Technology

Jerrold M. Grochow

YOURDON PRESS
PRENTICE HALL BUILDING
UPPER SADDLE RIVER, NEW JERSEY 07458
http://www.prenhall.com

To join a Prentice Hall PTR internet mailing list, point to:
http://www.prenhall.com/register

Library of Congress Cataloging-in-Publication Data

```
Grochow, Jerrold M.
   Information overload : creating value with the new
information systems technology / Jerrold M. Grochow.
      p.   cm. -- (Yourdon Press computing series)
   Includes bibliographical references and index.
   ISBN 0-527631-4 : (hc : alk. paper)
   1. Information technology.  2. Systems design. I. Title
II. Series.
T58.5.G76  1996
004'.36--dc20                                    96-31190
                                                 CIP
```

Acquisitions Editor: *Paul W. Becker*
Editorial/Production Supervision and Interior Design: *Dit Mosco*
Cover Art & Design Director: *Jerry Votta*
Cover Design: *Anthony Gemmellaro*
Manufacturing Manager: *Alexis R. Heydt*

Published by Prentice Hall PTR
Prentice-Hall, Inc.
A Simon & Schuster Company
Upper Saddle River, New Jersey 07458

The publisher offers discounts on this book when ordered in bulk quantities. For more information, contact Corporate Sales Department, Prentice Hall PTR, One Lake Street, Upper Saddle River, NJ 07458. Phone: 800-382-3419; Fax: 201-236-7141; E-mail: corpsales@prenhall.com

ISBN 0-13-527631-4

Prentice-Hall International (UK) Limited, *London*
Prentice-Hall of Australia Pty. Limited, *Sydney*
Prentice-Hall Canada Inc., *Toronto*
Prentice-Hall Hispanoamericana, S.A., *Mexico*
Prentice-Hall of India Private Limited, *New Delhi*
Prentice-Hall of Japan, Inc., *Tokyo*
Simon & Schuster Asia Pte. Ltd., *Singapore*
Editora Prentice-Hall do Brasil, Ltda., *Rio de Janeiro*

To Louise, Rebecca, and Joshua

Overview

Contents

Contents

Components Large and Small   *141*

Connecting the Components: Client/Server and Object Technology   *187*

Iterative and Incremental Development   *197*

Illustrations

Preface

The subject of this book is information systems development. It is about all the things that make systems difficult to develop using new technology. This is not, however, a "how to" technical book. It will not tell you explicitly how to avoid failures—and there have been many—or directly how to achieve success. It will tell you how to understand and use new information systems technology more effectively, a key ingredient in creating value for your organization.

This book is written for people who want to understand the technology that will be shaping the path of information systems development for the next decade. It is a book for people who need to know more about the issues that will be facing them in using the new information systems technology in their organizations; it is a book for people interested in practical advice on using that technology to create value for their organizations.

Many authors have written about the changes we are experiencing in all aspects of business and commerce. With the explosive growth of communication and information infrastructure, the global trading environment is subject to increasingly complex forces. Meeting the demands for information in this environment has led to the creation of complex information systems and complex systems development processes.

Over the past several years, myriad approaches, architectures, methods, and techniques have been introduced to deal with this increasing complexity (and cost), and I call these today's "new information systems technology."

Books have been written about each one—about client/server, about object technology, about patterns and frameworks, and about a multitude of others. Some of these books talk about successes and some about failures. Some of these books provide introductory material and some extremely detailed content—much more detailed than will this one. The goal of this book, however, is to serve as a guide as you attempt to make the connections among all these components of the new information systems technology, and to help you as you attempt to use them to create value for your organization.

The two major themes of this book correspond to two requisites of success with the new information system technology:

- Understanding the concepts of the new technology
- Implementing the technology to create organizational value

In focusing on the first theme, I introduce and describe the new information systems technology and discuss the interactions among the different concepts and strategies, i.e., the "components and connections." In dealing with the second theme, I discuss the significant factors affecting the use of this technology in a way that creates value for the organization. In pursuing both themes, I have tried to deal with several questions as each chapter was written:

- What are the key strategies of the new information systems technology?
- Where does the value come from in using each of the strategies?
- How do these strategies interact with each other in the process of creating value?
- How do we sort out that which will provide value from that which is just some technologist's toy?
- How do we decide when to bring new technology into our organizations, and then...
- What do we have to do to gain the value it is supposed to bring?

These questions are the subjects of this book. My purpose is to help you probe beyond the jargon to gain understanding of what the technology really means to the process of systems development and to the creation of value in the organization. Together, we will pursue the new information systems technology, explore its component parts, and then make the connections to find its broader implications for the organization.

READER'S GUIDE

Where shall I begin, please your Majesty? he asked. *Begin at the beginning*, the King said, gravely, *and go on till you come to the end: then stop.*

Charles Lutwidge Dodgson (Lewis Carroll)
in *Alice's Adventures in Wonderland*

This is a book about the implications of and interactions among the strategic components of the new information systems technology. Almost everyone involved in the use, selection, design, and implementation of information systems in large organizations will profit in some way from a few hours spent perusing its pages. This particularly includes executives making information systems (IS) decisions, IS managers or developers just getting started in the new technologies, and even "end-users"—those of you who actually use systems in your day-to-day activities. IS veterans already immersed in new technology will perhaps find the material little more than a compact review, but even they may glean a few ideas. Finally, I hope my readers include teachers and students of IS who are trying to understand how they can create value in the future from intelligent use of the new information systems technology.

Of necessity, this book deals with a number of technically complex topics and issues, but it is not meant to be a highly technical book:

- For readers with limited technical background, the book should provide enough information to allow you to understand how technology implementation issues will affect your organizations.[1]
- For all readers, it discusses technical issues in the broader context of business value that you will need to make decisions and resolve issues more effectively.
- For all readers, this book shows the connections among the components of the new information systems technology, and how they will be important to the systems in your future.

You will find a few quotations at points throughout the book where I have specifically copied the writings of other authors, and some places where I have borrowed from my own published articles. I have also included many citations that can be referenced by the interested reader, but since this is not an academic treatise, I have not attempted to provide a comprehensive literature search of all relevant material.

---

1. Where you see the ▼ after a section heading, you will know that this is a "technical backgrounder" for you to read. Of course, the more technically aware reader is welcome to peruse these sections as well, if only to recognize the definitions I am using for the jargon associated with the new information systems technology.

> ### CONNECTIONS: *Introduction*
>
> *Finally, you will find a number of places throughout the book where I highlight the connections among the different components of the new information systems technology. These paragraphs are preceded by the title "CONNECTIONS," as is this paragraph.*[2]

A WORK IN PROGRESS: CYBERSPACE UPDATES

While this book focuses on those topics that are likely to have the greatest impact on information systems development over the next several years, it is impossible to be complete and up-to-date in the medium of a printed book. In some sense, that makes this book a work-in-progress.

You have purchased a printed document at a point in time that will (I hope) give you insight into the issues involved in implementing new information systems technology. But the technology continues to change, as do the experiences and insights that will help you to be successful. We all have to find ways to continually update our knowledge and ideas, and I hope you will, therefore, want to go beyond the printed page.

As I update the chapters in this book or write additional essays, I will be putting them on-line, in "cyberspace." I would expect everyone reading this book (certainly by the time you finish it) to have access to the Internet and the World Wide

---

2. That wasn't quite the final point, but I wanted to put this one as a footnote. Sometimes when I write, I like to go off on rambling (or not so rambling) discussions of related (or not so related) points, or inject into the discourse what I believe to be some bit of humor. (I am told by certain of my colleagues that I sometimes do this in speaking as well. More often than not, these asides will include references to events that happened before some of my colleagues were born, so I understand their apparent lack of interest.) I have relegated most such asides to footnotes, although some will appear as parenthetical remarks if they are short enough. You can, of course, ignore them if you are attempting to hurry through the text. I will also use footnotes to reference other parts of the text, as in "see section such-and-such for further discussion." One of my reviewers couldn't stand seeing this type of "hypertext" link directly in the text, so I am forced to resort to footnotes due to a lack of better "technology." One of my other reviewers couldn't stand all the footnotes because he just couldn't bring himself to ignore them! Oh, well.

Web (which are also discussed in the book), so they are the logical place and medium to serve as my repository. I invite you to "visit" my home page by pointing your browser to http://users.aol.com/jgrochow and to send me e-mail with your comments. In this way, I hope to encourage further discussion of the ideas and issues I have introduced you to in this book.

ACKNOWLEDGMENTS

Although I wrote most of this book while on leave from American Management Systems, many of the ideas and some of the diagrams were developed in my work at AMS. I am indebted to the management of AMS for giving me permission to use them here, and to my many friends and colleagues who have contributed to them over the years.

I would like especially to thank those who directly assisted in the writing of this book, although none of them should be blamed for any errors or omissions. In particular, for research and administrative assistance, Mary Bowen, Nancy Gregory, and especially, my assistant Patricia Sitterson; for graphics, Henry Loutsenhizer; and for editorial review, Milt Hess (who for the second time labored long on my behalf), Tom Kosnik (of Stanford University, whose early comments redirected my efforts), Peter DiGiammarino (now of Hyperion Software), Fred Forman, Capers Jones (Software Productivity Research), Mark Raiffa, Charles Rossotti (Chairman of AMS), and Ed Yourdon (Yourdon Consulting).

And because every book-writing project is really a family affair, I would like to thank my spouse, Louise, and my children, Rebecca and Joshua, who were forced to spend all summer in exile in Chilmark, and my parents, who didn't expect to be mentioned here.

J.M.G., Washington, DC

The New Information Systems Technology

What is the new information systems technology? From the system developer's viewpoint, it is client/server, distributed computing, distributed data, and the like—the ways in which hardware and software systems components are connected. From the designer's viewpoint, it is objects, patterns, and frameworks—the building blocks that are used to construct those systems. From the end-user's viewpoint, it is PCs, windows, and networks—the physical evidence of the use of technology. And from the organization's viewpoint, it is ultimately the information that the technology processes and that helps the organization achieve its goals.

But it is even more than these: the new information systems technology is those additional concepts that support the creation of distributed object-oriented client/server systems—concepts such as strategic partnering, open systems, middleware, and architecture—that together are reshaping systems and systems development as we enter the twenty-first century.

The time has come, the Walrus said, to talk of many things...

Through the Looking Glass

CONNECTIONS: *Design Patterns to Components to Client/Server*

The activities performed in creating an information system include architecture, design, development, and implementation. When those activities employ new information systems technology, they are based on the concepts of patterns, frameworks, objects, and components. Although systems today often use only one or two of these concepts, more and more developers are embracing them all, from the creation of design patterns to their eventual use within the components of client/server systems. The new information systems technology is the coordinated use of all these ideas, concepts, and approaches.

More and more developers are making the connections among the components of the new information systems technology. And these are the "connections" that we will be discussing in this book.

1 Understanding The New Information Systems Technology

Client/server, object technology, components, and *patterns* are some of the terms used to describe the new technology of today's information systems. Understanding something about them—the hardware and software used to realize information systems and the techniques employed in designing and implementing them—has become a necessity for a very wide audience. End-users need some understanding in order first to participate in the development process, and then to avoid the frustrations of dealing with systems that don't always behave as they would like. System developers need more detailed understanding, of course, to make the technology decisions best suited to their projects and to their organizations. And top management—the CEOs, the agency directors, the partners—all need some understanding so they can deal with the system developers and end-users in their sometimes struggle to work together.

Beginning about 10 years ago, an increasing number of innovations in hardware, software, and development methodologies began to be applied to business and management systems. The decade from 1985 to 1995 saw an order of magnitude greater change in hardware, software, development methodology and tools, networks, user interfaces, and every other aspect of information systems technology than the two decades before it. And as far as we can predict, that pace is continuing—and perhaps accelerating—as we stand on the brink of the twenty-first century. Not only do we need to understand today's new information systems technology, but we need to be prepared for tomorrow's as well.

So, how should we define "the new information systems technology"? The definition has three parts:

"The new information systems technology" comprises those technologies that

(1) *are key topics at gatherings of information technology practitioners,*

(2) *are already used by some major organizations in some strategic systems,*

(3) *are still considered "leading edge" but not yet "mainstream" for the majority of organizations.*[1]

In applying this definition, we need an anchor or central theme. For this book, it is client/server. Client/server is what all the fuss is about. It is a result of a major rethinking of the way in which computers can work together to process information. Client/server computing has caused us to totally rethink not only the hardware architecture of systems but the software architecture and our development processes as well. Even the latest in Internet and World Wide Web technology is based on the client/server approach. Although client/server isn't necessarily less expensive to implement than older technology, it provides new capabilities and flexibility that the older technology could not.[2] Client/server is really where the new information systems technology begins.

---

1. What is new for one organization may be old for another; or perhaps it is so new that it is too far out even to consider, so the particular selection of technologies in this book certainly invites discussion or even argument. That's fine, but keep in mind this definition as you read the remainder of the book.

2. From a McKinsey study of 20 companies and why they adopted client/server: "Although we did find some examples of client-server systems being used to replace obsolete, expensive-to-run minicomputers and mainframes, most of the systems we encountered had been chosen because they could do things that mainframe systems could not. Either they provided new capabilities, or they allowed systems to be developed more quickly — or they did both at once. Cost savings, when they did occur, came as a bonus." [Beyer 1994]

> ### CONNECTIONS: *Client/Server, Components, Objects, Frameworks and Patterns*
>
> *Client/server systems are constructed from a variety of components—hardware and network components such as PCs and "server" computers, software components such as operating systems and business applications, and a hundred other programs in between (so-called "middleware")—some off the shelf, some requiring a great deal of programming and development. In more and more cases, the software components are composed of "objects," modular units following specific design and programming rules. Objects may be grouped into "frameworks" that implement broader-based functions (e.g., GUI frameworks, database interface frameworks, and accounting frameworks). And those frameworks may have been based on a "pattern," a written description of a particular way of implementing a common function.*

Typically, the end-user of a client/server system is interacting through a fairly sophisticated "graphical user interface," with graphics and pictures appearing on a computer display screen as well as text. The end-user employs a variety of input devices ranging from a keyboard and pointing device (mouse, trackball, electronic pen, touch-sensitive screen) to speech and, in the future, gestures.

Underlying (or overlaying) everything is the concept of systems architecture, taking an architect's point of view (in addition to that of a designer or a builder) of the system and its development. In fact, the study of how patterns are used to construct frameworks of objects, which are then combined into a component-based client/server system, *is* the study of systems architecture.

The system development life-cycle most often used in developing client/server systems approaches design and development as an iterative process where the system is delivered incrementally. With client/server systems, developers have recognized the difficulty of following a linear "specify-design-program-test" approach, especially when they use new technology to introduce new functions to a volatile business environment.

The new information systems technology is thus a combination of several ideas that together provide a strategy for implementing systems (see Figure 1). Although this figure shows a

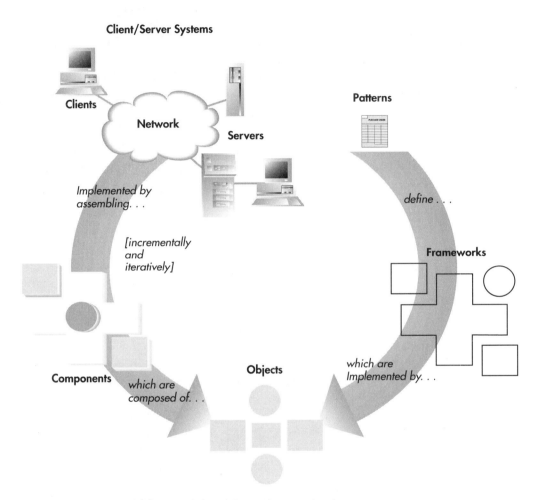

Figure 1: Components of the new information systems technology

common portrayal of the relationship among the ideas and strategies of the new information systems technology, it is not always this simple. You can implement client/server systems without taking an iterative approach, without using object technology, or without using any of the new information systems development approaches. You can use patterns, frameworks, and even objects in implementing systems that are not client/server.

But the greatest business benefits from the use of new information systems technology come from the combined use of most or all of these concepts. In fact, it is difficult to talk about one without talking about the others: client/server architecture, object frameworks, component construction—the words always seem to be run together. And that is why you have to understand what they are all about. I hope this book will provide you what you need to know.[3]

---

3. But don't expect this section to replace a library of books or a lifetime of study: it is a review framed in the context of components and connections. For continuing education, you might also try cyberspace. Check out the Internet User Groups (USENET) *comp.client-server* and *comp.sw.components* as well as numerous World Wide Web sites.

2 Other "New" Information Systems Technology

The list of technologies that could be included in a discussion of new information systems technology is long and getting longer every day. I have chosen for discussion in this book those that are both central and pervasive to almost all strategic systems development or will become so in the near future. Each of these technologies has actually been available for at least two decades, although many have only recently seen widespread use in strategic business systems.

There are other technologies whose role in information systems development is somewhat less central but nonetheless likely to have a major impact in certain classes of systems in the remaining years of the 1990s. As usual, they are the subjects of multiple books in their own right, and they are listed here as a signpost for further study. The brief mention I give them should indicate nothing more than my inability to include every important topic in this one work.

- *Artificial intelligence:* using various software and hardware approaches to mimic human understanding and behavior, e.g., knowledge-based systems and neural networks.
- *Data warehousing and mining technologies:* approaches to collecting and analyzing data to improve operations and create new opportunities for the organization.
- *Network technologies:* different approach to implementing wide-area networks.

- *Groupware technologies:* strategies that encourage collaborative work, as exemplified by Lotus Notes.[4]
- *Workflow:* analysis of business processes to yield flowcharts of process interactions, both computerized and manual, and the software to automate those interactions.

The list goes on...

---

4. The PC world continues to be driven by a series of products that take the entire industry to new levels of sophistication. The introduction of Lotus Notes products is almost single-handedly responsible for the increase in knowledge management systems, sometimes called groupware systems. Going back to 1979, it was Visicalc, the first spreadsheet, that turned the Apple II from a hobbyist's toy to a business machine that could solve real-world problems. Lotus 1-2-3 is said to have had the same effect on the IBM PC just a couple of years later. The PC became the tool of choice for processing words as well as numbers with the introduction of inexpensive but robust word processing software (Microsoft Word and Corel's WordPerfect), which was also responsible for the demise of the special purpose word processing computer earlier popularized by Wang Computer and Digital Equipment Corporation (both of which took years to recover from this and other setbacks). Some products took longer to work their magic, but it is reasonably well accepted that Novell's local area network operating system has been a key factor in the decline of the mainframe computer as a stand-alone computing solution. And Notes is responsible for changing information into knowledge that can be made available to thousands of people across the enterprise. What will be next? No one really knows for sure, although World Wide Web servers and browsers are clearly in the lead. It would be suicidal to assume that we have seen the last of such seminal products, however, and bet on the status quo.

The Value of New Information Systems Technology

You may be among those who are skeptical of the value of new technology—and you would be right to have your skepticism. We have seen the introduction of many new computer systems technologies before, but where have they gotten us? We still have systems plagued with excessive maintenance costs, IS departments with unfathomable backlogs, and more than our share of system development failures.

The new information systems technology does not in and of itself create value for an organization. Intrinsically, there is no greater or lesser value in client/server technology than in mainframe system technology. The value comes from the ways that new information systems technology allows us to create systems that have higher value to the organization.

> *There are no technical decisions, just business decisions.*
>
> Dawn Lepore, executive vice president and CIO, Charles Schwab & Co., "Quote of the Week," *Information Week*, April 8, 1996

Understanding the new information systems technology, although a prerequisite to creating high-value systems, is not sufficient. We have to use that technology effectively in implementing systems that create value. We have to introduce that technology in situations that make sense. We have to acknowledge that effective use of the technology carries with it implied changes in procedures and organization (without which it is basically worthless). We have to deal with the many technological factors, but recognize that it is the management factors that most often determine success or failure.

Beginning in 1990, I led a team of the best systems architects at AMS[1] in developing an architectural and development strategy that would update the "foundation software" approach our organization had been using for a decade.[2] It was quite an advanced strategy for its time and had served (and continues to serve) AMS and our clients well. We were concerned that its roots were in a time when the mainframe reigned supreme, and that just wasn't the way computer systems would be built in the years ahead. We explored numerous ideas and techniques, and we quickly concluded that object technology (among other related ideas) was more than a passing fad and was likely to be very important to our industry. In giving a progress report to our company chairman (this was definitely a project with "top management backing"), I apparently spent a little too much time talking about object technology and its expected impact on the development process and the structure of systems. The chairman interrupted me and said, "Stop talking about objects and start talking about business benefits." He was right, and I never forgot it.

---

1. American Management Systems has been my employer for more than two decades. AMS is a business and information technology consulting firm whose mission is to "partner with clients to help them achieve breakthrough performance through the intelligent use of information technology."

2. This approach has been talked about at many conferences and meetings and was documented by my colleagues Dr. Fred Forman and Dr. Milton Hess in [Forman 1988].

Charles Wang, chairman of Computer Associates, in his excellent book on the relationship between information systems and business executives, notes that:

The CEOs had little use for CIOs [Chief Information Officers] who lose sight of the business when dealing with technological decisions. [Wang 1994, p. 26]

The key to achieving value with the new information systems technology is to keep sight of the organization's business objectives. Whether the issue involves information systems internals and is of interest primarily to the IS organization, or whether it involves the creation of systems to support a new business venture of interest to the CEO, the decision criteria can be framed relative to the organization's goals. Unfortunately, too many information systems professionals attempt to answer questions on why they are using new information systems technology by launching off on the efficacy of client/server architectures and the number of MIPS or gigabytes or BPS that the system can handle. They fall into the trap of answering what they thought was a technical question when what was really being asked was a business question. When you connect the technology to the business objective it is supposed to achieve, that is when the new information systems technology creates value for the organization. That is when it is time to introduce new technology—assuming, of course, that the business value of doing so outweighs the costs.

Sometimes, it is simply a matter of presentation. Introducing a new technology because it will allow the organization to serve 10,000 additional (and profitable!) customers is a business reason; introducing a new technology because it will allow the IS department to create a system that can handle 2000 transactions per hour is a technical reason—but ultimately they are the same reason. In the first statement, "organization" is the object; in the second it is the IS department—and that makes all the difference. IS managers who say that "our organization has to move to new technology to stay competitive" are voicing a business reason, even if they think they are simply dressing a technical reason in business clothing. If customers won't do business with you because they perceive your organization to be behind the times, then new information systems technology has a very direct business value. Focusing on your organization's customers is key in making today's executives "hear" your arguments.[3] The issue is to look at the strategic reasons for implementing new technology as well as the tactical or implementation reasons.

Object technology and the other concepts of new information systems technology provide value through the systems they are used to develop and the capabilities that those systems provide to the organization. What we have come to learn is that new technology in and of itself is valueless. New technology used in pursuit of a business vision has value. New technology that enhances the value of the processes carried out by the organization takes on the value it helps create.

---

3. I know that it is in vogue to talk of "clients" rather than "customers" (clients are customers who keep coming back), but I thought it would be too confusing in a book that spends a lot of time talking about clients and servers. By the way, you don't have to be a profit-making business to have customers or clients. All organizations have customers—as governments, universities, and other non-profits started realizing not too long ago—and they are all working very hard to turn them into clients.

3 How Does The New Information Systems Technology Create Value?

Michael Porter in his book *Competitive Advantage* [Porter 1985-1] discusses the "value chain" of activities in a firm that result in its products and services. He focuses on the need to examine the interactions among those activities to understand "the behavior of costs and the existing and potential sources of [competitive] differentiation." Porter talks about primary activities (materials handling, manufacturing, packaging, distributing, marketing, sales, and services) and support activities (procurement, technology development, and firm infrastructure) that transform inputs (raw materials, human resources, and technology) into outputs. Information systems are part of *every* activity since "each value activity also uses and creates information."

In Porter's view, the value of an organization is what people are willing to pay for its goods and services. Therefore, the new information systems technology creates value when it enhances the value of those goods and services. It can do that in several ways (see [Porter 1985-2]). When the systems we create with the new information systems technology...

"create competitive advantage by giving companies new ways to outperform their rivals...

"change industry structure and, in so doing, alter the rules of competition...

"spawn whole new businesses, often from within a company's existing operations..."

then truly, they have created value for the organization.

Federal Express's package-tracking system is an example of a new system changing the entire concept of products and services and thus the competitive structure of an industry. Federal Express created value with technology by equipping its delivery personnel with hand-held computers that could communicate (via a radio in their trucks) with the customer service system. This gave FedEx the ability to provide an entirely new level of customer service, directly tracking packages at every step of the delivery process. This approach is now the standard in the industry, and it has created tremendous value for Federal Express as the leader and innovator.[4]

Other examples are found in almost every industry...

...from *banking* (the ATM which redefined the idea of a branch bank and significantly lowered the cost of delivering key services)

...to *telecommunications* (automatic call directors coupled to automatic number identification which created the capability for comprehensive telephone marketing and customer service)

...to *automotive manufacturing* (equipping cars with computers to make them more efficient and provide new capabilities to drivers such as anti-lock braking)

...to *state government* (public access computer kiosks that created a new relationship between government and the body politic).

Some are major innovations, some minor, but all are examples of new technology introduced to create value for their organizations. Some contribute directly to revenue-generating activity. Some increase customer business in businesses where revenue isn't the measure (e.g., non-profits, governments, universities). Some systems enable increased productivity or decreased operational costs.

Expanding on Porter, an Arthur D. Little study cited these ways in which information technology can help create value for the business [Band 1994]:

---

4. Of course, systems also create value when they reduce the cost of providing the goods and services of the organization. This is also a valid value, but Porter was focusing on the revenue side of the ledger.

- streamlining the business
- responding rapidly to changing market conditions
- responding more rapidly to customer requests
- using resources more flexibly and economically
- innovating more quickly
- expanding breadth of product line
- improving total product quality
- competing for and serving customers on a global basis

These are all ways in which systems enable, support, or directly create value for their organizations.

The Forrester Research organization believes that establishing a direct link between corporate revenue and profits is a requirement for the future, and this requires a focus on the organization's customers:

> *"By focusing efforts on the new customer connection, IT will prove its value in measurable terms that business executives care about—new revenues, new customers, and new profits. The result will be a direct link between ITs value and future budget levels— and a vastly more important role for IT." [Forrester 1995]* [5]

But some systems create value in indirect ways, and that is important too. Even the most mundane change to an existing system affects the organization in some way. Each change has the potential to increase or decrease costs as well as to increase or decrease competitiveness. If a new user interface makes it more difficult for payroll clerks to do their jobs in assisting employees, the ramifications can be felt in both increased costs and, eventually, decreased competitiveness as employees become frustrated in carrying out the mission of the organization. How many times have you been served by frustrated clerks saying "the computer fouled up" or "this new computer system doesn't allow us to do that" and vowed never to do business with that organization again? Or, contrarily, found that the organiza-

---

5. While I generally applaud this statement, I don't think it is necessary for IT (or IS) to have a "vastly more important role," but rather to fulfill its role effectively in improving the ways organizations deal with their customers.

tion had saved enough information about you and your transaction to make doing business with them easy—for you as well as for them?

All of the situations presented above are the direct result of computer system changes—some positive, some negative—that affected the organization and its interactions with its customers. Many are the result of someone within the IS department having introduced a new information systems technology and having created value (positive or negative) in the process. What we need to do is make sure we understand the process well enough so that the value created is positive more often than it is negative. We have to understand specifically what the value-creating effects are, how and when they occur, and then how to manage them.

3.1 THE SPECIFIC EFFECTS

Let's deal specifically with the components of the new information systems technology: how do they create value? Some examples have just been given: hand-held computers, ATMs, and computer kiosks are all examples of *advanced user interface* technology used in *client/server* systems. While we didn't talk about how these and other examples were developed, some of them undoubtedly employed *object technology* and were constructed from *components* and *frameworks* based on an *application architecture*. They are all examples of systems employing the new information systems technology in creating value for their organizations.

But exactly how did these systems create value? In some cases, they created value by making possible new business services that customers found valuable. The Federal Express system provided a highly marketable new business service (instantaneous package tracking) via a client/server system with the "client" in the truck and the "server" at a central location. Customers found it very valuable to know where their packages were when they hadn't yet made it to their destinations. This capability clearly led to increased revenues and increases in the number of customers served. It could not have been done without employing the new information systems technology.

The new information systems technology make possible the systems that create value. The new user interface allows the customer service representative to answer more of the customers' questions more promptly. Object technology allows the organization to modify its systems more quickly to beat or meet changing market needs. Component construction allows those same systems to be upgraded quickly as improvements in computer systems technology permit improvements in speed, access, or costs. Figure 2 provides examples of these and other ways that the new information systems technology provides the means to create value.

Figure 2: The new information systems technology creates value

Technology Approach	Kind of Value	How Value Is Created	Example
Client/server	Improved customer service	Provides multiple sources of information to customer service representative	Equitable Life's customer service system
Client/server	New products and services	Allows new types of applications via local computer processing and communicating with central databases	Frito-Lay's field agent support system
Client/server; advanced user interfaces	Increased revenue via employee empowerment	Allows field personnel to provide more service to customers	Hand-held and mobile computer ordering applications
Advanced user interfaces	Expanded employee capabilities	Allows new classes of end-users by making the computer easier to use	Iowa State Police accident tracking system
Advanced user interfaces	Decreased cost	Reduces paper, provides multi-user access to files	USAA's paperwork imaging system

Figure 2: The new information systems technology creates value (Contd)

Technology Approach	Kind of Value	How Value Is Created	Example
Object technology	Decreased cost	As a development technology, increases productivity of developers and reduces cost of maintenance. As a design process, improves communication between developers and end-users, thereby reducing need for rework	Strategic systems of all kinds; Brooklyn Union Gas's billing and customer service system
Object technology	Increased competitive flexibility	As an architectural strategy, allows rapid response to changing needs for system functions	Banking and securities industry systems; billing and settlement systems
Iterative and incremental development	Decreased cost	Allows better communication of system functions between developers and end-users thereby reducing need for rework	Strategic systems of all kinds
Component construction approach	Increased competitive flexibility	Improves response time of IS by permitting more rapid replacement of modules	Strategic systems of all kinds

3.2   (IS) Reasons for Introducing New Technology

So, if all reasons ultimately come down to helping the organization fulfill its mission to its customers, where do we start, and how do we make that connection? The full chain of reasoning can start almost anywhere: it can start with some technologist going to a seminar that extols the virtues of objects and components; it can start with a vendor pitching a new type of middleware; it can start with the leader of the organization playing golf with a leader of another organization and talking about technology. It should result in achieving higher productivity in the IS department (an OK reason, but not "customer focused"); providing new capabilities to personnel in the field (better); or being able to serve more customers more completely (best). This is where it should end up—and quickly.[6]

The most common reasons for introducing new information systems technology are to:

- improve short-term productivity in the IS department,
- improve long-term productivity in the IS department,
- increase flexibility in upgrading hardware and networks to meet changing capacity requirements,
- improve the ability to maintain application systems so that change requests can be satisfied more easily,
- improve the capability to respond to future technology changes,
- improve the usability of applications, and
- improve the responsiveness to changing business needs.

Although all of these will have an impact on the organization's ability to serve its customers, none of them actually mention that fact.

Goldberg and Rubin asked respondents to their surveys to give the top reasons why they chose object technology for their

---

6. Yes, this still happens—and more often than you may realize. Unfortunately, too many technology upgrades are started on the basis of "how come we don't use client/server, object technology, components, [insert your favorite technology buzz word here]?" Too many end in failure to brand this a desirable starting point.

projects. Almost all were presented as IS reasons rather than business reasons:

- Reduce development time; reduce amount of software to create (13 projects)
- Participate in state-of-the-art technology, apparent market momentum (9 projects)
- Improve long-term maintenance (8 projects)
- Use what a prior project used (5 projects)
- Create desired GUI, especially for accessing a database (5 projects)
- Improve system structure to help organize applications (4 projects)
- Obtain design consistency (3 projects)
- Obtain better user involvement; enable customers to configure systems (3 projects)
- Improve ability to evolve the [software] product, handling the rapid pace of business change (3 projects) [Goldberg and Rubin 1995, p. 59]

Where is the business purpose? Where is the customer? Where is the value to the organization?

The reason for introducing new information systems technology is to create systems with added value for the enterprise. Here is how the IS department should be using the new information systems technology to do just that:

- by providing easier-to-learn, easier-to-use computer systems to end-users so that they can do their jobs more efficiently and effectively;
- by responding quickly to changing business needs so that the organization can better satisfy its existing customers and attract new ones;
- by creating systems that enhance the existing businesses of the organization or allow it to expand into others;
- by working with managers in other departments to help them understand something of the new information systems technology and what it can do; and

- by training its own staff in the ways that new information systems technology creates value.

The point is that information systems managers must begin to think in the same terms as line managers. What is the purpose of the organization? Who are its customers? How is what I am about to do going to help them (directly or indirectly)? When we all start answering these questions, we will find that all the "IS reasons" become business reasons—or else we are working on the wrong problem.

CONNECTIONS: New Information Systems Technology and Business Value

Here is the key connection: developing systems using iterative and incremental techniques, constructing them using objects and frameworks, and architecting them with modular client/server hardware and software will allow the IS department to respond quickly with valuable systems. We have the technology to meet the demands that are being placed on us; now we have to use it effectively to meet those demands.

4 Balancing Risk and Reward

Even if there are good business reasons for introducing new information systems technology, many other factors enter into the decision-making process.[7] For example, there is the issue of risk: you can be *sure* that you are taking on significant risk by employing new information systems technology, but can you be sure that the organization is equipped to handle it?

In the past, new systems were justified on the basis of a cost-benefit analysis: when would the benefits derived from the system pay back the costs of developing and maintaining it? Costs were calculated and balanced against the sum of tangible benefits (such as reduction in operations personnel) and intangible benefits (improved access to data would result in improved decision making). Every calculation was an estimate, of course, but with a reasonable assurance that they were sufficiently accurate to use in decision making.

---

7. Although one could argue that all factors should be accounted for in the determination of business value, it is quite hard to do this in a practical sense. While it would be nice to think of all decisions in terms of comparing a single number ("the business value"), attempts at creating this number (as, for example, by creating weighted averages of factor importance times factor value) fall far short of the mark. Only in the rarest cases (i.e., those with the greatest positive-to-negative swing in possible outcomes) is it really worth it to analyze the many dependencies among the different factors and the many approaches to how weights and values for these factors should be determined. Attempting to create a single number on which to base all information technology decisions is a case of summarizing a process beyond the point where the important information has been lost. The important differentiators will have been so homogenized that the "just right" solution appears to result when it is actually the average of some "too hot" and some "too cold" ideas. See Section 38.3 *A Balanced Scorecard Approach to Measurement* on page 239 for discussion on how I think value should be measured.

With new technology (especially for the first such systems being developed in an organization), cost estimation has become much more difficult. By the very definition of "new," we don't have a lot of experience to fall back on in developing our estimates.[8] Furthermore, there is little or no data to quantify expected benefits such as productivity increases from graphic user interfaces or object technology, or the value of having "more flexible systems" that the new technology is supposed to provide.

To these difficult issues of cost-benefit analysis, we now add the issues of risk:

- What is the risk (probability) that the costs will be significantly more than we had estimated (so that we wish we had never started the project!)?
- What is the risk that the (however tenuously) calculated benefits will not materialize?
- What is the risk that the benefits won't be benefits at all?

While it goes without saying that the appropriate time to introduce new technology is when the expected rewards meet the organization's criteria for being higher than the costs, these criteria must include a variable to cover risk.[9] Are the expected rewards *sufficiently* higher than the expected costs to account for a high risk that those expectations may not be met?

That is the difficult question: when are the costs, rewards, and *risks* appropriately balanced for your organization? The following discussion focuses on this balance.

---

8. I did a survey of object technology gurus a couple of years ago regarding estimation of system development costs, only to find that the consensus technique was "estimate it like you would a COBOL system and it will be less"—hardly a satisfactory approach.

9. It should go without saying, so why am I saying it? Perhaps because I have seen too many organizations that seem to ignore this aspect of the analysis.

4.1   "FOLLOW THE CURVE"

As with many phenomena, both physical and sociological, the adoption of new technology across the population tends to follow a normal distribution, the familiar bell-shaped curve shown in Figure 3. With time on the horizontal axis and number of people (or organizations) adopting the technology at a point in time on the vertical, Rogers [1983] distinguishes people by when they enter the fray:[10]

- Innovators (first 2.5%)
- Early Adopters (next 13.5%)
- Early Majority (34%)
- Late Majority (34%)
- Laggards (16%)

Innovators are the venturesome. They are willing and able to try some things that won't work. Early Adopters represent the group that sees value from being among the leaders in adopting something new. According to Rogers, "this adopter category is generally sought by change agents to be a local missionary for speeding the diffusion process." Laggards, at the other extreme, wait until most of the world has already proven the technology before they will try it. In reality, there is a group after Laggards, "Never Adopters," the group that for one reason or another never uses the particular technology being studied.[11]

While a bell-shaped curve describes the technology adoption behavior of organizations as a group, it does not explain the underlying forces governing that behavior. In particular, two prime motivators seem to come up again and again in discussions of technology adoption:

---

10. Many authors have adopted and modified Rogers's classification. For example, James Martin, a prolific author in the computer field, calls the categories "early adapters" [sic], "pragmatists," "late adapters," and "resisters" [Martin 1992]. These categories seem to carry a somewhat more pejorative terminology than Rogers's, however.

11. One reason is because they were so late in adopting the technology that the competition forced them out of business.

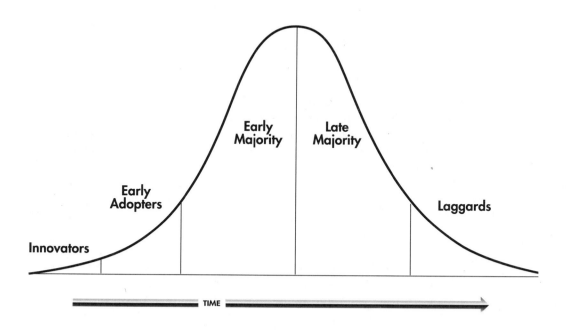

Figure 3: Technology adoption curve

- *Risk*, i.e., what and how much risk is being taken (that the outcome will not be as expected), and is it justified by…
- *Reward (Advantage)*, i.e., what advantage is there to adoption at that point in time, and what is the payoff?

Risk and advantage need to be looked at separately and as dependent factors. You might think that your tolerance for risk is independent of other factors, but it isn't. For example, you might say that you are willing to accept a certain level of risk ("normal business risk") in introducing a specific new technology. If you thought that it was imperative for the competitive success of your organization to be using that technology, you might be willing to take on significantly more risk than usual. In other words, your interest in taking on risk is influenced by your assessment of the level of competitive advantage you would achieve (or, in the negative sense, advantage you would lose relative to your competition). The reverse works as well: if there was little or no competitive advantage, you might not want to take on any risk at all. Risk and competitive advantage are, therefore, dependent factors in making a decision to introduce technology.[12]

4.1.1   Portfolio Theory of Risk Management

People and organizations will not necessarily follow the same adoption strategy for different technologies. In some cases, they will act as Innovators, in others, as Early Adopters, and in others, perhaps even as Laggards (unlikely, but possible). In fact, a reasonable argument can be made that total risk to the organization is reduced (and competitive advantage increased) by taking different approaches, i.e. by viewing your technology investments as a portfolio to be managed to acceptable risk and reward levels.

This type of analysis parallels the strategies of money managers in creating financial portfolios. Depending on the degree of risk you are willing to tolerate, they can create portfolio strategies with different expected rates of return. The same is true with new technology: taking a significant risk on one technology might perhaps be balanced by taking less of a risk on another (i.e., waiting until later in its maturity cycle). Alternatively, it might make sense to "spread your risk dollars around" by making smaller investments in each of several approaches rather than a large investment in only one.

In reviewing the sections that follow, keep in mind that one technology decision is not necessarily independent of another, if you are trying to maximize the total value of all new technology to the organization.

4.2   THE RISK CURVE

It is often assumed that the adoption curve also corresponds to a "risk-taking" curve, with Innovators taking the most risk, Early and Late Majority taking reasonable risk, and Laggards taking the least risk. In the case of technology adoption, this doesn't necessarily hold true. While Innovators are clearly taking the most risk, Laggards are also taking on significant risk. Innovators

---

12. There is a large body of mathematical and organizational theory related to decision making and the way in which different factors can dependently or independently operate to influence the decision-making process. A classic work is [Keeney and Raiffa 1976].

risk that the technology is immature and poorly supported, making it difficult for them to be successful in implementing or using the technology. They also risk that the technology will not be well received in the market and will be supplanted by another technology, thus forcing them into another high-cost decision. Examples in this category include the ADA programming language and many computer-aided software engineering (CASE) tools. By waiting until the end of the adoption cycle, Laggards are taking the risk that the technology has reached its decline or even the end of its economically useful life and that they, too, will be forced into another high-cost decision.[13]

Take, for example, the organization that is beginning to develop new mainframe systems in 1996—they will find that their risk of not being able to maintain this system (and get the value from their investment) is quite high. Vendors do not want to enhance software, and programmers do not want to take jobs maintaining software that is viewed as outdated and that has a declining market. Indeed, Late Adopters of client/server (i.e., those still developing mainframe systems) may be taking on as much risk as the Innovators! Figure 4 portrays the risk of technology adoption as almost an inverted bell, starting high and declining, but then starting up again somewhat later in the life-cycle of the technology.

---

13. I make the distinction between "end of its useful life" and "end of its economically useful life." Many organizations continue to use technologies beyond the point where it is economically appropriate to do so and end up losing to their competition.

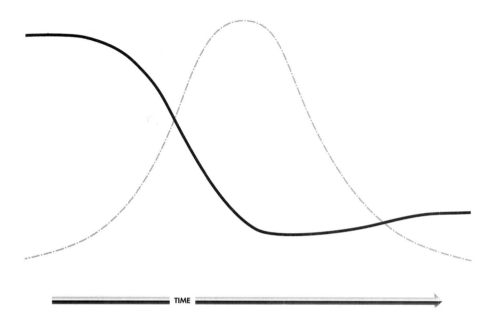

TIME

Figure 4: Risk related to technology adoption curve

4.3 THE REWARD CURVE

Just as we can graph risk versus time, we can graph reward. There are two general types of rewards from being an early adopter of new information systems technology:

- Achieving some type of competitive advantage (providing a new service via equipping field personnel with hand-held computers, providing better customer service via integration of computer and telephone technology, or perhaps being seen as a "technology leader" in an industry where that translates into increased business).

- Achieving the business payback sooner (by developing a client/server-based restocking and order entry, a major retailer might project savings of over $1 million per week— so they want to get started on development sooner rather than later even given the risk).

In the former case, there is likely to be a relatively short period in which you can truly achieve competitive advantage. In the package delivery industry, it is now almost impossible to achieve competitive advantage with package-tracking technology—if you don't have it, you aren't in business! Predicting the shape of the competitive advantage curve then becomes very important. In Figure 5, we show one type of competitive advantage curve overlaid on a typical technology adoption curve. There is a strong competitive advantage from being among the early adopters in this case, although the advantage is somewhat less from being too early (when the value of being first is not yet realized in business benefit).

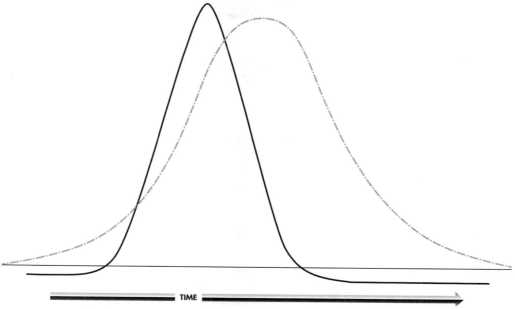

TIME

Figure 5: Competitive advantage related to technology adoption curve

4.4 BALANCING RISK AND REWARD IN ADOPTING NEW TECHNOLOGY

The issue as to when to adopt a new technology is not just risk, but the reward that accrues as well. The relationship of risk to reward and their absolute magnitude are the considerations likely to govern your actions, or at least influence them a great deal.

When Federal Express became an early adopter of hand-held mobile computer technology [Margolis 1990], they were in part making a decision that the potential reward (of increased business by providing better service) justified the risk of becoming involved in a relatively new technology. When Brooklyn Union Gas developed a new customer service system using home-grown object technology, it was making a decision that the expected additional payback of jumping in at that time would more than offset the risk of being among the first organizations to take this approach.[14] It was trying to achieve the twin benefits of increased development productivity in creating a system with very high flexibility to respond to an increasingly dynamic business environment. It was betting that use of the object approach, a very new technology in the business community, would provide payback; it would allow the company to create a highly flexible system to satisfy changing regulatory needs, and to gain competitive advantage by identifying and servicing new customer segments. It was a system that might even have been impossible with a less risky approach or if it had been delayed until a later point in the life-cycle of object technology.

Figure 6 shows both risk and competitive advantage curves overlaid on the technology adoption curve. If we divide the horizontal axis into four sections, we can discuss the implications of being at different points on the technology adoption timeline.

- The leftmost section is the Innovators, those who are not particularly deterred by the risk. They are the ones likely to be using a new technology because it is new or because they perceive the reward to be higher and to be achieved sooner than most other people perceive it to be.

- The second section, the Early Adopters, are the ones most likely to achieve competitive advantage on a consistent

---

14. The Harvard Business School case study on this project [Andersen 1992] is one of the few sources to note that the decision to try object technology was made while BUG (interesting initials) was in the middle of a major strike, management was literally out in the streets fixing gas lines, and the project team (reduced to five people) for the New Customer System was trying to figure out how to keep things going. This was in 1986 when BUG must have been fairly desperate to find some way of getting to a new level of programmer productivity. In this case, necessity was indeed the mother of invention.

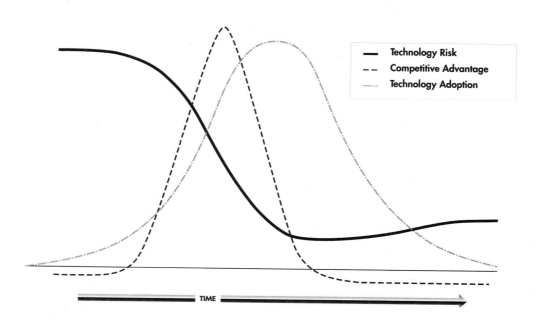

Figure 6: Risk and advantage related to technology adoption curve

basis from their use of new technology. The risk has started to come down as the results of the Innovators' use become known and solutions to problems become available. The value of using the technology is a little easier to determine as well. Early Adopters are sufficiently out in front of the pack that they will reap the benefits when the majority of organizations are just starting to look for them.

- The third section, comprising the Early and Late Majority, have a lower tolerance for risk and are willing to sacrifice some of the reward in order to sleep better at night. They will do well also, but not if they are in highly competitive situations.

- Finally, the fourth section is where the unsuspecting Laggards begin to use the technology, assuming all is well, that their risk is minimal, and that this is the approach that will hold them for years to come—a seemingly reasonable strategy, but not one that will succeed in a world increasingly driven by innovations in computer technology.

Of course, there is a significant problem for corporate decision makers in trying to create a chart like this to describe a particular situation. Determining the dimensions of each curve as well as their relative placement would require data that can at best be obtained only approximately (and only then at some expense). Finding specific data to answer questions such as...

- how significant is the competitive advantage from using a specific technology at each point in time?
- how significant is the risk?
- over what time period will the risks be reduced to lower (more acceptable) levels?

...is beyond the realm of the typical analyst and moving into the world of the fortune teller. Luckily, what organizations need is to be approximately correct rather than exactly wrong.

4.5 BALANCING RISK, REWARD, AND READINESS IN ADOPTING NEW INFORMATION SYSTEMS TECHNOLOGY

What is the optimal point for bringing in a new technology to achieve the desired relationship of risk to reward, i.e., risk to competitive advantage? Or, where do the risk/reward curves overlap in a way that maximizes your risk/reward ratio? Balancing technology risk and reward, however, is often not a sufficient criterion for determining when to adopt a new information systems technology. Organizational readiness (or organizational risk) is another factor that will affect the success of your efforts.

At AMS, we have prepared an extensive checklist of organizational readiness criteria [Best 1994] with the major categories of:

- technological readiness (status of infrastructure—hardware, software, network; technology decision-making apparatus; prior attitude toward new technology; etc.)

- organizational/cultural readiness (technology management structure; approach to decentralized decision making; risk tolerance; etc.)
- senior management readiness (level of understanding of new technology; commitment to effective use of new technology; general expectations; perceived urgency; etc.)
- staff readiness (skills; ability to assimilate new technology; tolerance for organizational change; etc.)

Questions are asked as part of a readiness assessment with the goal of placing the organization on a "ready-not ready" scale for each item.

The Gartner Group has weighed in with its own view of client/server readiness and has published several strategy papers on this topic. Its categorization includes:

- strategic readiness (What is the business strategy that requires client/server technology?)
- IS readiness (Is the IS department ready to take on development and operation of client/server systems?)
- financial readiness (What is the source of the money to bring in client/server?)
- end-user readiness (Do the end-users understand what this is all about and how their roles in development and operations, as well as end-users, will change?)
- technology readiness (Will the available technology support the system scope and size that you envision?)

Regardless of whose method you follow, you can display the results graphically to highlight where you are and where you have to be. A "radar" diagram[15] such as that shown in Figure 7 is one effective way of showing multi-dimensional data you will have collected. Each hemi-axis (there are eight in this diagram) represents one factor in overall organizational readiness. Plot the value of a particular factor on a scale where the center of the

---

15. This is the name used in Microsoft Excel, but it is also known as a "spider diagram" or a Kiviat Plot after Philip Kiviat, who first popularized its use in the information systems community (dozens of examples can be found using one of the Internet search engines).

diagram is the least favorable value and the outside is the most favorable (1 to 10, low to high). Once you have plotted a point on each axis, shade the area enclosed by connecting the points. The ideal situation of highest organizational readiness would be depicted by a shaded disk covering the entire area out to the ends of the axes (the example shows a more typical situation!). This diagram provides a quick way to assess your current situation as well as to plot improvements over time (using different colored shading, for example).

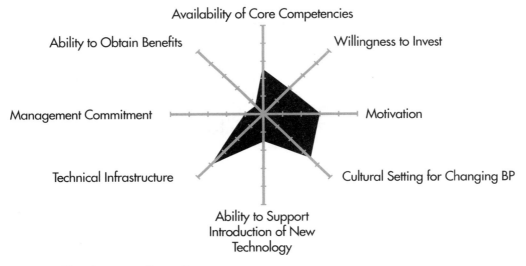

Figure 7: Client/server readiness diagram

There are too many dimensions of organization readiness to adopting a new information technology strategy for you to ignore the readiness assessment. Your organization will be in a much better position to decide on a course of action once you have collected readiness assessment information and highlighted the results. Those results can be translated into tasks aimed at improving your readiness and lowering your organizational risk. Compared to the cost of implementing new information systems technology, the readiness assessment is but a small insurance policy.

5 A Strategy for Using New Technology to Create Value

"

Would you tell me, please, which way I ought to walk from here?

That depends a good deal on where you want to get to, said the Cheshire Cat.

I don't much care where —, said Alice.

Then it doesn't matter which way you walk, said the Cat.

Alice's Adventures in Wonderland

"

Ah, but it does. Walking in the wrong direction, i.e., taking the wrong approach to adopting new technology, rarely results in success. Even given the right reasons for using new information systems technology, you cannot be successful if you don't follow the road signs—and obey the traffic laws.

- You can't introduce new technology into an organization that doesn't want new technology.
- You can't force end-users to like new technology if they don't see the business value.
- You can't spring a new system on people and expect them to accept it as their own.

In short, you can't expect to create value with new technology if you don't have an appropriate strategy for doing so. Here are some basic steps to follow in implementing that strategy.

1. *Determine readiness of the organization to adopt new technology.*

Assess the organization's position on the risk-reward-adoption curves. Make sure that the key executives are on board for the level of risk.

2. *Develop a concept for the business processes that incorporates the use of new information systems.*

Based on your knowledge of the capabilities of new technologies, determine how they can be used effectively in implementing new or improved business processes.

3. *Determine whether the use of new technologies is integral to the business process.*

Make sure you aren't just taking a "new technology for new technology's sake" approach. Can you get the same improvement without taking on the risk of the new technology?

4. *Create a plan for implementing the systems that allows for adjusting the concept and the approach.*

Remember that no one is really smart enough to predict all the effects that the new technology is going to have. Make sure that your development process allows for incremental development and iteration toward its conclusion.

5. *Prototype the system and show the results to the end-users, keeping them involved in the implementation process.*

Part of the iterative/incremental approach means that you should be producing prototypes of your system that can be verified with end-users. If you want them to "own" the system, they must be participants in its development, and there is no better way to do that than by getting their feedback on prototype after prototype.

6. *Incorporate measurement criteria into the plan to allow analysis of the impact of the new systems, i.e., to determine how they created value.*

When all is said and done, you want to be able to show that the new technology was important after all. Start with some idea of how you are going to measure that, and it will be a lot easier to draw an appropriate conclusion.

John Seeley Brown, chief scientist at Xerox Corporation and a noted thinker on introducing new technology into organizations, said the following (paraphrased, in [Bollier 1993]):

1. Focus more on relationships than on things. Information technology can and should change relationships among people, that is where its chief value lies. Information technology that changes the nature of relationships can change the fundamental features of a given complex system.

2. Honor "emergent behavior."...Therefore, information technology should allow the emergence of competing...models... and enhance their interrelationships.

3. Under-design systems in order to let new truths emerge... "Don't set forth some a priori notion of truth or design in totality (which requires an infinite intelligence in any case). Use intelligence to under-design a system and assist the emergence of new ideas)."

You want to get the benefits of new technology in implementing new systems that will help the organization meet its objectives in a constantly changing world. If you follow the road signs, you are sure to get there—without walking longer than you have to...

—so long as I get somewhere, Alice added as an explanation.

Oh, you're sure to do that, said the Cat, *if you only walk long enough.*

All New Systems Are Client/Server Systems

Client/server, distributed processing, two-tier, three-tier—we can invent more terms than we can possibly use appropriately. And, in fact, we often do not use them appropriately or consistently. We have converged on the term *client/server* as the commonly used label for any computer "system" requiring more than one computer to get the job done. Regardless of where the data or the processing or the objects reside, if the system involves a computer on your desk (or your work table or in your hand) communicating with another computer (via a wire or infrared or radio-frequency waves), you can call it a client/server system.[1]

There are surveys (weekly!) that purport to tell us what percentage of today's systems are client/server systems and what the intention of the typical IS shop is for creating more. The July 1995 *CIO Magazine* reported on an industry survey recently completed by Deloitte & Touche showing that 58 percent of all systems in operation used client/server architecture and that this would rise to 66 percent in 1996 [Plewa and Pliskin 1995].

These statistics prevail in spite of the difficulty of implementing client/server systems. Client/

---

1. This is, of course, a "popular" definition. You can use it with impunity, at least among non-academics, many of whom still adhere to the more stringent definitions of *client/server* (actually a software architecture in which a "client" asks for service from a "server" regardless of whether they are both physically on the same machine).

server systems are generally more complex than systems operating on a single computer, involve more interactions among components supported by different vendors, entail more risks of software or hardware incompatibilities, have more performance and reliability problems, and require more sophisticated "decentralized" management and support. With all of these difficulties, they must provide something of great value or organizations (at least the rational ones) would shy away from them. Difficulties can be surmounted, although at a significant cost, and organizations large and small are embracing client/server as the architecture of today and the future.

And this is the key point: in most organizations, in government, industry, or the non-profit sector, almost all *new* development activities are directed to the creation of client/server systems. Even in those cases where the computers on the desk are communicating with the mainframes in the glass houses, they are creating client/server systems. And that is why I say, for all practical purposes, *all* new systems are client/server systems.

6 More Definition ▼

Until the mid-1980s, the vast majority of computer applications required only a single computer to perform their functions completely. The end-users of these applications generally required a lot of training (and re-training) because of the complexity of the "user interface," i.e., the arcane codes that end-users were required to remember and type into a typewriter-like computer terminal. In the quest to improve the user interface, designers and programmers recognized that they could provide much more sophisticated interaction by using personal computers as the interface to other, typically more powerful, computers running the remainder of the application (the "business function" and the database). This was the first step to "client/server": the PC became the client of the larger computer acting as the server.

Over the past several years, system developers have devised a variety of ways for programs and data to be divided among multiple computers. Sometimes the programs are split ("distributed"), sometimes the data, and sometimes both. The wide variation in client/server applications raises numerous questions about why, what, and how to distribute. And that is what makes it all so complicated.[2]

In an interesting article on critical information systems technology issues, Benjamin and Blunt

---

2. It may not appear that complicated, but it is. The issue is who sees that complication: the end-user (hopefully not!), the application programmer (too often), or the "middleware" developer. Several years ago, when we were working on some of the first production-quality client/server systems, we had to do all the middleware programming ourselves (i.e., we had to create adjuncts to the operating systems to allow our applications to be partitioned across multiple machines). Today, hundreds of vendors will be more than happy to sell you their products to handle these functions. Of course, that situation presents its share of problems as well. See Chapter 24 *The Component Approach Creates an IS Technology Supply Chain* on page 160.

[1992] provide a succinct statement of the key reasons for the growth of client/server computing:

The distribution of processing will be driven by the economics of computation and telecommunications and by the need to fit processing into organizational work patterns—none of which favor centralized processing. Integrity in large multi-location applications will still demand that master data and updating processes be stored at one or at most a few locations.

Client/server computing is growing because of the combined impact of the economics of computing and the needs of the organization. Changes in both factors favor a decentralized (multiple computer) rather than a centralized (single computer) approach, and that is what client/server is all about.

6.1   DEFINING THE CLIENT, THE SERVER

They also serve who only stand and wait.

John Milton, "On His Blindness," 1652

By common usage, the computer that has the end-user interface is most often called the "client" and all other computers are called *servers*, e.g., application server, communication server, database server.

This nomenclature is not always technically correct, however, and some client/server gurus prefer to apply the term "server" appropriately to whatever *process* is doing the serving, wherever it resides. In fact, a particular piece of hardware may have software running on it that performs client functions in one case and server functions in another (e.g., a computer serving as an "application server" is almost always also a client of a database server). And, to really confuse the issue, many UNIX configurations have the end-user's computer acting as a graphics/window server to application clients running on other computers. Of course, all this does is point out the possibility of confusion and provide another reason why it is important to see a connectivity diagram (or two or three) to find out what is really going on.

7 "Drawing the Line"

Before discussing the "how" of client/server, we must understand the "what." Many different classification schemes have been proposed, and most follow a basic form. They begin with a simplified diagram of the structure of a typical application system, as in Figure 8. This rudimentary "architecture" diagram is the basis for discussion about the types of client/server systems.[3] This diagram breaks the system into three components:

- *user interface functions*, including all input and output directly to the end-user;
- *application functions* or processing, referring to the programs doing the "work" of the application; and
- *data access functions*, programs that control access to the databases (the database management system, interface routines, and any editing or integrity control programs).

To round out the application environment, the diagram also shows:

- the *end-user workstation* and
- the *database.*

The partitioning of an application into user interface, application processing, and data access is one of the key bases for creating highly flexible applications, as we will show later. It is also one

---

3. Architecture is the topic of a major section of this book, but I introduce the topic only briefly here. See *Architecture Is the Answer; What Is the Question?* on page 81 for a lot more detail.

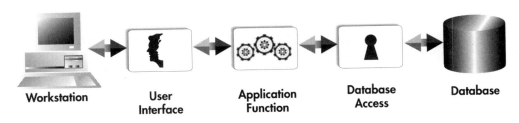

Figure 8: Application structure

of the bases for labeling some client/server applications "three-tier" applications.[4]

Creating a client/server application can now be viewed as drawing a line or lines to show which parts of the application will operate on which computers. The type of client/server processing depends on where you draw the lines.

- If you don't draw any line, i.e., everything operates on a single machine, you don't have client/server, i.e. the entire application on a computer local to the end-user (hence, the term *local processing*).
- If the user interface is on a workstation and everything else is on other computers, you have *distributed user interface*.
- If significant parts of the application function are split between two or more computers, you are in the *distributed application* mode.
- If the key databases and associated processing are separate from the application function, you have *distributed data access*.
- If significant portions of the database are split between two or more computers, you have a *distributed database*.

---

4. See Section 7.2 *Two-Tier vs. Three-Tier Architecture* on page 51.

Figure 9 shows this classification scheme. Classifications can be combined so that, for example, you can have an application with both distributed function and distributed database.

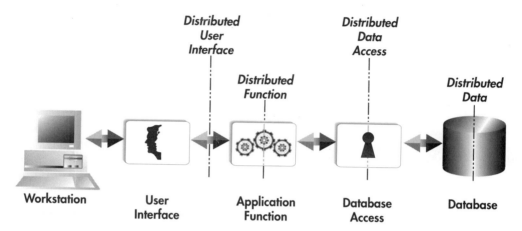

Figure 9: Modes (types) of client/server computing

This analysis is an expansion of one first published by Alan Scherr in the *IBM Systems Journal* in 1987 [Scherr 1987] in which he defined four "modes" of distributed processing. Since the system can actually be partitioned in many different ways (that is the lines can be drawn almost anywhere), the classification of client/server systems requires almost a continuum rather than the discrete four, five, or six types that most authors describe.[5]

One often-referred-to classification scheme is published by The Gartner Group (see [Bradley 1994]). It shows five types of client/server computing (see Figure 10).

---

5. Of course, those authors know they are providing a simplified discussion so that we don't go completely crazy in trying to talk about how our systems are architected. Furthermore, the basic classification scheme and the terms I have used are not uniformly applied. Rather than accepting a particular label as describing a client/server system, you need to see a diagram of its specific architecture. To this end, I advocate the use of several diagrams rather than one to represent the different aspects of a client/server system's architecture. See Chapter 13 *Defining System Architecture* on page 83.

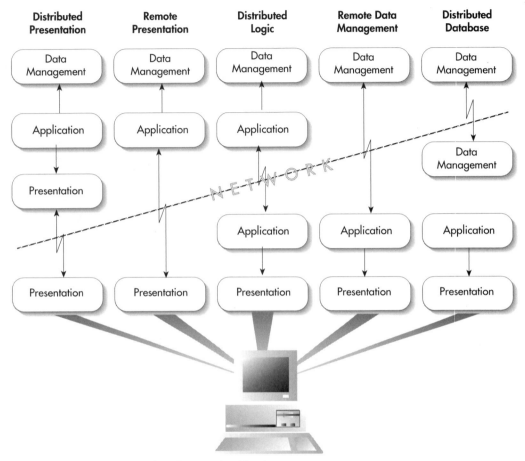

Figure 10: Gartner Group client/server classification

7.1 "DRAWING THE LINE" AS AN ARCHITECTURAL ISSUE

How do we decide where to "draw the line?" How do we determine the best client/server architecture for our applications? Each approach makes trade-offs among criteria such as operational performance versus operational costs, flexibility and scalability versus development costs, and reliability versus capital costs. Each of these criteria will have different importance to different applications, each will have different values at different points in time, and each will result in a different type of client/server system.

A *distributed data access* system (where a database server is accessed from remote computers), for example, will allow you to have much better control over data security than a *distributed database* system (where the data itself is split over multiple computers), especially if some of the data is distributed to individual workstations. Flexibility will also be enhanced via distributed data access since the database server is the only machine that needs to be changed if volume increases. There may also be better tools available for managing a distributed data access network than there are for managing distributed data. However, system performance may be lower and communications costs may be higher using distributed data access, because each request will require a response from the database server machine. In a well-designed distributed database approach, many data requests will be able to be handled locally (i.e., on the same machine initiating the processing). Given the potentially unlimited number of ways in which distribution decisions can be made (i.e., lines can be drawn), for each system you develop, you should list and evaluate the specific criteria that are important to your application. However, you should keep several general principles in mind.

- It is always faster for programs to access data or other programs locally (on the same machine) than to access them on a remote machine via a network.

Client/server designs have to balance the effective use of multiple computers with the cost of communications flowing among them and the system performance (response time and throughput) that results. The greater the communications necessary among the different parts of a client/server application, the slower that application is going to appear to the end-user. Speed and cost of processing and communications must be evaluated together when making client/server architecture decisions.

- If applications are CPU-intensive, the total time to move data around the network and perform the processing remotely will be faster only if the remote computer is significantly faster than the local one.

This basic fact has led to such innovations as the high-powered graphics workstations from Silicon Graphics and "mini-supers," small computers with the processing power of super-computers but without other large system capabilities (i.e., high input-output bandwidth or expansion capabilities).

- Distributing even a small amount of data (such as static reference data) creates a distribution management problem.

Maintaining the same data on multiple machines (i.e., replicas) presents significant management problems. While most relational database management systems today provide replication capabilities, those capabilities often have limitations (such as allowing only server-to-server replication).

- Distributing application function (and even user interface function) to hundreds or thousands of desktops creates a significant management problem.

Keeping program releases synchronized across a large network of computers has proved to be one of the continuing nightmares of client/server operations departments everywhere. One reason for the popularity of World Wide Web technology is its ability to download fresh copies of user interface and application programs every time the end-user accesses them, thus eliminating this problem. If you are going to distribute application function, make sure that you include the management issues as part of the cost-benefit analysis.

Another point needs to be made about flexibility. Not enough is known about the performance characteristics of client/server to ensure that a design will work exactly as planned. Actual use of the system will also deviate from the assumptions made by the designers. Further, the cost and performance characteristics of computers and networks are subject to significant changes over the life of a system. For these reasons, flexibility is an extremely important criterion in distributed systems. Ideally, you would like to be able to determine dynamically where the various applications and databases reside, or at least be able to make changes without having to modify programs. Some client/server development tools and approaches allow this type of flexibility; others do not, as many system developers have discovered.

Portions of this section are based on material in [Grochow 1991]

7.2 TWO-TIER VS. THREE-TIER ARCHITECTURE

In today's parlance, the terms "two-tier" and "three-tier" refer to types of client/server architecture. A two-tier system is one in which the user interface and application processing are integrated, but the processing associated with the primary databases is separate; or alternatively, the user interface is separated from integrated application and database processing. Three-tier systems are those where the user interface and application processing have been further separated to increase modularity and flexibility. The user interface, the application processing, and the database processing are the three (separate) tiers.

This definition doesn't say anything about the number of computers involved in the application, although that is often implied. In a two-tier system, the user interface and application run on one computer, and that is networked to the database server running on another. In a three-tier system, an application server is additionally separated from the computer operating the user interface (typically the PC on the end-user's desk).

These definitions of two-tier and three-tier are the current usage. Only a few years ago, the number of tiers was often used to refer to the number of "levels" of database that existed in the system: if data were maintained on the desktop, on a mid-level database server, and on the mainframe, then the system was a three-tier system. This definition has fallen out of use but sometimes reappears just to cause confusion.

In an architectural sense, the important point is the separation of different types of processing (user interface, application, and database) to increase modularity and flexibility. You can, of course, modularize even further and create multi-tier systems. Why restrict yourself to having only one tier devoted to the application function, particularly if it makes logical sense to split it further? Why limit yourself to having the database in only one tier when it may make sense to split it among desktop and multiple servers (as in the "old" definition of three-tier)? Today's client/server systems are becoming more and more modularized in both senses of the use of "tiers."

The definition of "n-tier" is hard to pin down. Once again, the architecture of the specific client/server system cannot be determined from a simple label, and we have to look at the architecture diagrams to see what is really going on, as in Figure 11, a multi-tier application with user interface on the desktop, database on two computers (database server and enterprise server), and application processing on three (desktop, application server, and enterprise server).[6]

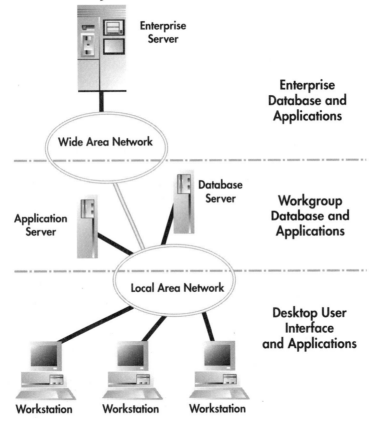

Figure 11: Multi-tier client/server architecture

---

6. The software (development tools and middleware) to implement multi-tier client/server and multi-tier distributed databases is available, but is somewhat limited and fragile. You may find that it takes a Herculean effort to ensure reliable operation in a high volume, 24 x 7 environment. At some point, the complexity of n-tier distributed possibilities exceeds the ability of the designer, developer, and maintainer to keep control of both application and data.

7.3 FAT CLIENTS, SKINNY CLIENTS

In all client/server development projects, developers have to decide how much processing to put on the desktop or "client" computer and how much to put on the various server computers. If you put a lot of processing on the desktop, you will need a big machine there—a "fat" client. If you put most of your processing on the server, you will need (presumably) a smaller machine on the desktop—a "skinny" client.

In many two-tier client/server configurations, the desktop machine has to support a sophisticated user interface as well as the application function. This takes a powerful machine—sometimes more powerful than the end-user has available. In today's terms, this means a Pentium-based PC (or equivalent) with 16Mb main memory, several hundred megabytes of disk storage, and a high-resolution display. This so-called "fat client" approach often drives the cost of the client/server system beyond economic feasibility for the system and necessitates a review of the basic architecture.

Enter three-tier client/server to reduce the processing load on the desktop and move it to the server. Reducing the processing requirement on thousands of desktops (which would otherwise have to deal with the "peak load" for each and every end-user) and replacing it with increased processing load on tens or even hundreds of servers is often a better solution. And, as previously noted, you don't have to move all the application processing to the application server if it makes sense to keep some of them on the desktop (for response time reasons, or because only a few end-users need particular functions).

The issue of the "fat client" versus the "skinny client" is taking on a whole new dimension with the advent of the World Wide Web and use of this approach to client/server on the Internet as well as within the organization for so-called "Intranets."[7] One of the key advantages cited for Web technology over other approaches to implementing client/server is the fact that it can enable sophisticated applications without creating inordinate

---

7. See Chapter 11 *The Impact of World Wide Web Technology* on page 70 for a more complete discussion of these topics.

demands for processing power on the desktop. In some cases, using Web technology would appear to reduce the client-side processing requirement below the capacity of today's basic personal computers. This has spurred some hardware manufacturers (and one database manufacturer) to announce the production of what I call the "anorexic client," a machine that can do little more than connect to a network and run a Web browser. Since none of these devices is available at the time of this writing, we will have to wait and see whether this becomes a viable computer architecture for use in strategic business applications.

8 A Legacy System to Client/ Server Migration Strategy

One of the best ways to show how client/server technology is being used today is to trace the steps in a possible strategy for migrating a mainframe application to new technology. In terms of creating business value, this migration strategy often has a significantly higher benefit-cost ratio than throwing the existing (or so-called "legacy") system out and starting afresh with new technology.[8] We begin with the system schematic in Figure 12.

An important business driver for client/server is to provide more sophisticated user interfaces that are easier to use and learn, e.g., that use windows, icons, graphics, etc.[9] This leads quite logically to "front-ending" the mainframe application with a PC that provides the desired user interface, as shown schematically in Figure 13. The PC provides the end-users with a new system, or at least one that is significantly different in look and behavior from what they have had before, while providing the mainframe with exactly the input it expects to receive from a character-based terminal. When this type of client/server system was first implemented in the early 1980s, PCs actually had add-in electronics to emulate the physical characteristics of typical mainframe terminals.

---

8. It is interesting that we most often refer to existing mainframe systems as "legacy systems." A more complete definition might be that "a legacy system is one that is difficult and costly to maintain and enhance but still provides the organization with needed functionality." It is regrettable that many of the client/server systems being implemented today will become legacy systems tomorrow.

9. The usual abbreviation applied to the standard graphic user interface is WIMP which is discussed in Chapter 33 *Windows, Icons, Mice, and Pull-downs: The Graphic User Interface (GUI)* on page 216. The system developer who came up with this pithy mnemonic "clearly had no idea" (right!) of its homonymic implications.

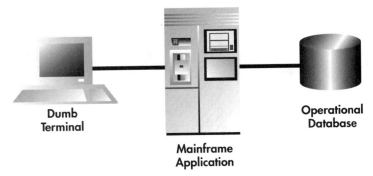

Figure 12: Basic mainframe architecture

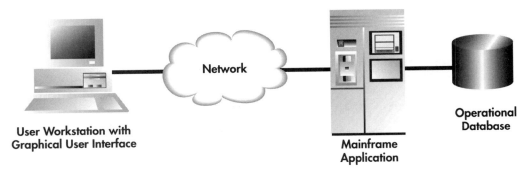

Figure 13: Mainframe application with GUI front-end

Later, both PCs and mainframes were updated with electronics that allowed connection via local and wide-area networks. In the early 1990s, several software vendors offered development environments specifically for implementing this type of system, and many of those systems are still in active use today.[10]

Getting access to the millions of pieces of information locked up in mainframe databases is another major business issue that IS shops are attempting to deal with via client/server technology. While many inquiry tools are available for accessing data directly on the mainframe, they are often characterized by slow speed, high operational cost, and limited features. Client/server provides an alternate solution via databases and inquiry tools

10. Of course, many of those tool developers went out of business as this style of client/server system was superseded by others. The issue of third-party vendor stability is addressed in Chapter 25 *Selecting Components* on page 173.

running on PC or UNIX-based platforms. The level of sophistication of these tools (at least for inquiry usage) and their cost advantage relative to mainframe tools makes this a very attractive architecture.

The simplest way to develop a client/server database inquiry environment is to create an extract program that periodically copies data from the mainframe to a database server running one of the many SQL database management systems. More sophisticated data updating approaches involve real-time (or near real-time) data "replication" as well as the application of various data manipulation functions (coding changes, file merging, etc.) before the server database is created. When multiple data extracts are collected from the operational files of multiple applications and organized into a structured database, that database is often called a "data warehouse."[11] Figure 14 illustrates this concept.

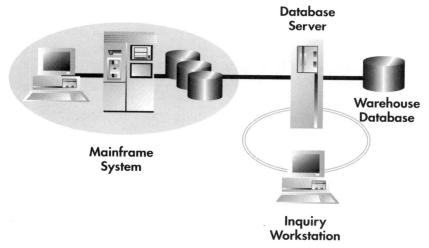

Figure 14: Back-end data warehouse added to mainframe application

---

11. As with any jargon phrase, many vendors will claim that existing products provide data warehouse capability. Although there are many products that do provide capabilities for creating and accessing data warehouses relatively easily, *caveat emptor* clearly applies. This is yet another example of how our industry sometimes jumps on a term-of-art and reduces it to such a common marketing term that it loses much of its meaning.

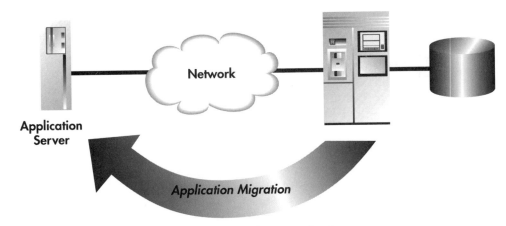

Figure 15: Application server connected to mainframe application

Some would argue that you do not have true client/server systems until you have put a significant application function "on the network" (see Figure 15). In the case of existing mainframe systems, it often does not make sense to take a piece of the application and run it on a separate computer as an "application server." It might make sense to do that if that portion of the application were really in need of major revamping (as, for example, if major new functionality had to be added to meet business needs, governmental regulations, or competitive pressures). In that case, the new functions (or revamped old functions) would be developed in a new environment and connected with the mainframe via the network. This approach typically does not require major revision to non-affected parts of the mainframe system and can be the beginning of a pragmatic introduction of client/server computing.

Another approach to migrating mainframe applications to client/server environments is to implement a so-called "downsizing" strategy. Under this strategy, most or all of the application function is ported "as is" to computers that provide higher capability for lower cost or have other desirable characteristics, something that is often possible in the technologically innovative computer hardware industry (see Figure 16). Most often, this approach is linked to moving CICS COBOL applications from their mainframe homes to UNIX-based machines running CICS emulators, or in some cases CICS itself. In spite of recent

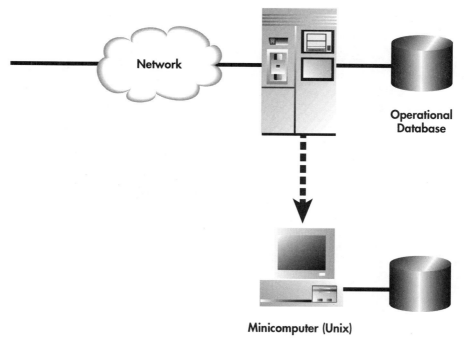

Figure 16: Downsizing a mainframe application

cost analyses showing that client/server environments are more expensive to maintain than mainframe environments, this strategy makes economic sense where network infrastructure (including support) is already in place and the cost issue is primarily the price of mainframe usage versus the price of hardware to operate the equivalent system under UNIX—which in today's market is invariably significantly less.

Finally, it is possible to combine all the approaches we have just discussed, adding GUI front-ends, data warehouse backends, migrating some functions to separate application servers, and migrating whatever is left to a downsized machine (see Figure 17). You can create client/server applications in a variety of ways and in a variety of forms, starting from scratch, or starting from your existing mainframe application—it all depends on what your real business needs are.

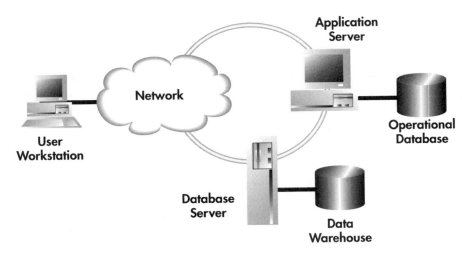

Figure 17: Completed client/server conversion

9 All Projects Are Systems Integration Projects

Organizations employing the new information systems technology in a client/server system will of necessity become aware of the supply chain that produced that system. We do not yet know how to hide the fact that a client/server system is constructed from components supplied by multiple manufacturers, both hardware and software, and that all the parts do not go together smoothly. When we buy a toaster we know it is built from components, but the vendor of the toaster has effectively eliminated our need to know this. When we buy an automobile, a much more complex product with many more components, this is also true (at least if we continue to use the original dealer for all maintenance work).[12]

The differences between legacy and client/server system environments in this regard are significant, as Figure 18 shows.

---

12. Of course, many of us choose to learn about individual components and the range of suppliers, particularly when it comes to tires, batteries, and other easily replaceable items. However, the choice is ours: we can always go back to the dealer and treat the entire vehicle as a single unit, ignoring its component structure to save time and effort.

Figure 18: Component environment vs. legacy environment

Legacy Environment	Client/server Environment
Mostly "integrated" structure	Mostly "componentized" architecture
Few "visible" components	Many "visible" components
Components typically ancillary, e.g. system management	Components integral and critical
Components generally independent of one another	Components often inter-dependent
Many other organizations using the same combinations of components	Few (if any) organizations using same combinations of components
Infrequent releases/updates to individual components	Frequent releases/updates to individual components
Synchronized releases/updates to individual components	Independent releases/updates to individual components
Good/excellent vendor support	Fair/poor vendor support

Not too many years ago, you could buy an entire system, hardware and software, from a single company (typically IBM or Digital Equipment Corporation). Today, that is next to impossible—and the result is that all systems project become "systems integration" projects. Whether you are developing the system within your own organization or using a third-party system integrator, you will be involved in the effort to bring together the various components of your system (there is only so much of this effort that you can delegate to others). "Open systems" not-withstanding, you will have to put significant effort, first, into selecting those components, then, dealing with interface incompatibilities, less-than-optimal vendor support, decisions on when (or whether) to upgrade to new releases, and a variety of other problems.[13] These are the difficult tasks that distinguish a systems integration effort from a more traditional system development project.

---

13. Many of these topics are discussed in other sections; See Section 10.1 *Standards and the Myth of Open Systems* on page 67, Chapter 16 *Proving the Technical Architecture* on page 107, Section 16.2 *Dealing Effectively with Upgrades and New Releases* on page 110, and Chapter 25 *Selecting Components* on page 173.

CONNECTIONS: *Client/Server, Components, and Open Systems*

Client/server systems are obviously (too obviously) composed of multiple components and, despite attempts to create "open systems" standards, those components require a significant integration effort.

Successful client/server projects will recognize the inherent systems integration tasks that must be performed. They will often have a separate team or task track charged with the responsibility of bringing together the various hardware, software, and network components. These tasks must often be accomplished in parallel with development of the application code, and that will cause task dependency problems. For example, developers will begin to produce code that assumes certain releases of component products, such as class libraries or reporting tools. If the systems integration team finds some reason to change to a different release (which they invariably will—usually to make two products work together), the application developers will often find themselves re-coding, perhaps redesigning, and certainly re-testing. This problem can rapidly escalate to changes in database management systems and even underlying operating systems, with consequently larger involvement of the application developers.

While these problems might argue for performing many of the system integration tasks after initial code is developed, that approach is a sure path to missed deadlines and cost overruns. Whatever rework must be done due to systems integration changes found during application development will only be worse if the changes are not discovered until after application development is nearly complete. As rework mounts, the project will be further and further behind schedule—and open itself up to even more integration problems as vendors begin to provide fixes and new releases to deal with other issues.

The need to perform systems integration tasks in parallel with other systems development tasks can be compared with the move to "concurrent engineering" in manufacturing. Traditionally, new products were designed by engineers, who then turned them over to production experts to figure out what components to produce and how to manufacture them (or buy them), who then turned things over to service experts to figure out how to maintain them. In the concurrent engineering approach, all experts are involved from the beginning, with frequent interactions among parallel teams, to design a product with the joint goals of being manufacturable, maintainable, and marketable. The analogy to client/server systems is to have the systems integration team (which performs the role of the production experts and service experts) working in parallel with the application team toward the goal of producing a system that is useful, reliable, and maintainable. In client/server development, systems integration is a continuous process, and it must be begun as early as possible in the project.

10 What Do We Mean by Open Systems?

The definition of open systems has changed several times since the term first came into vogue in the early 1980s. Back then, talking about "open systems" meant talking about inter-computer communications using the seven-layer architecture of the Open Systems Interconnect model specified by the International Standards Organization. Since not too many people were interested in the esoterica of communications proto-cols, this fairly limited and generally unsatisfactory definition was quickly superseded.

Over the next part of the decade, "open systems" were synonymous with "UNIX systems": if your system ran on UNIX, it was open, and if didn't, it wasn't. (See the cartoon on the following page.) Specifically, an open system was supposed to run on a UNIX version that followed specifications developed by the Open Software Foundation (OSF), an organization dedicated to establishing an "open" standard for the UNIX operating system (which really meant a standard not owned by AT&T). Since most versions of UNIX available at the time did not adhere to the OSF standard (and still don't), the definition of open systems quickly became broadened to mean "any system capable of running on some version of UNIX." Anyone who has used UNIX knows that this didn't mean quite as much as it might have because software that ran on, say, Sun's version of UNIX didn't necessarily run on HP's, at least not without some amount of rework. It is only recently, with the UNIX "branding" program of the X/Open Consortium (another industry group)

DILBERT ©1996. United Features Syndicate.   Reprinted by Permission.

The UNIX operating system and its gurus have always had a certain cachet among the develper community, as often evidenced in our humor, brought to you with permission—and the payment of a huge fee :)

that we are beginning to see real application compatibility across versions of UNIX.[14]

As the 1990s dawned, we were beginning to see major changes in the computer industry. IBM's dominance was being called into doubt. New companies were coming and going at an ever increasing rate. And CIOs were pulling out their hair and losing their jobs over what to do about it all. It was fairly clear that what everyone really wanted was not to worry about which hardware or software vendor they were using for their operating systems, their DBMSs, or anything else: what they wanted was "open" systems—systems where you could use components from different manufacturers as readily interchangeable parts. Open systems were systems where you had a choice about which vendors to use for various components, where you weren't locked into proprietary hardware or software architectures, where you could change your mind and your vendor without having to throw everything out and start all over. Open systems were systems whose components interfaced in standard

14. Even that may not be enough, however. X/Open has recently announced another branding program for the GUI associated with a UNIX system. Their Common Desktop Environment (CDE) is reported to have more than three million lines of code that vendors can incorporate into their UNIX systems. The jury is still out on how many UNIX vendors will incorporate CDE, with Digital, Hewlett-Packard, IBM, Novell, and SunSoft among those committed, but with Santa Cruz Organization saying they have no plans. More information on X/Open and UNIX branding is available on the Internet via the World Wide Web at http://www.xopen.org.

ways, and where those standards weren't controlled by a single company.

The story continues...

10.1 STANDARDS AND THE MYTH OF OPEN SYSTEMS

Material in this section is adapted from [Grochow 1996].

Open systems are a noble goal, but their pure form is mostly a myth.

The statement of the problem is deceptively simple: we want systems using components that adhere to a set of interface standards so that any component—hardware, software, user interface, digital media, or whatever—can be swapped out at will for a like component that claims to follow the same standards. We want components that can be switched with other components for zero cost (or very close to zero cost).

Achieving this, however, is insidiously difficult.

Open systems, by definition, are based on standards. Standards come into being either through a long-drawn-out process based on discussion among many participants from academia, the computer industry, and end-users as to what is best, better, or at least acceptable (such as a language standard), or through the very simple process of almost everybody using the same "thing" to do a particular task and accepting whatever it is as the standard (such as the Windows API for graphical user interfaces). We have numerous examples of both types of standards in our industry—and of almost every hybrid in between.

The problem, however, is that our industry thrives on innovation, and innovation is, by definition, non-standard.[15]

It is an annoying paradox: computer users and developers see the value inherent in standards, but also of the innovations that our industry keeps coming up with. It is unfortunate that anyone doing something innovative will of necessity be doing

---

15. Our industry also thrives on competition, and competition means that it is to a company's advantage to lock you in to their products, or at least make it very costly to switch—exactly the opposite of what consumers may want. Unfortunately, the stock market seems to value companies with a strong competitive position (read: "lock ins") more highly than those without it, so we have an additional obstacle to overcome on the way to open systems.

something non-standard, and that, by definition, isn't "open." SQL provides a prime example. All relational database vendors assure us that their products adhere to the ANSI (American National Standard Institute) standard for SQL. But they also tell us how they have added extended features that go beyond the standard, that allow us to get better performance, that allow us more flexibility, that allow us to move forward in using the latest techniques, that make each of their products different from the others.

To be truly open, you have to be mired in the past (or at best be in a very slowly changing future—after all, even standards get changed), and that locks you out of even more value than the use of standards provides. In fact, one of the reasons that we have so many standards being developed for the same type of interface (e.g., GUI, network, distributed function call) is that different groups are sure that they know how to do it better than everyone else if they could just get everyone else to listen to them (witness the OLE vs. OpenDoc debate, or the OMG vs. Microsoft scuffle over object request brokers). This locks us into a seemingly unending debate over non-standard standards and which emerging standard to use—or to wait for.

So there we have it: truly open systems and truly standard standards are an impossibility in the computer industry (at least until some company establishes a monopoly over all types of software and hardware, and we all know that could never happen...). The best we can do is to implement some standards, lobby for lots of interoperability, and play those market forces to our best advantage.

CONNECTIONS: Patterns, Frameworks, and Open Systems

As time goes on, we will see the adoption of more and more standards based on the work of standards organizations and committees. The movement toward component construction of systems (which is really a movement toward open systems) will force the creation of additional de facto standards. Sure, it would be a lot easier if we could agree on just one interface standard for each type or classification of component needing interfacing (such as objects or remote procedures or GUIs), but we can't and we won't. The recent interest in patterns and frameworks[a] is encouraging because it also implies interest in open systems. The more patterns and frameworks we all follow, the closer we will move to truly interoperable, exchangeable components. And that is what we really want and need.

a. See Chapter 23 *Patterns, Templates, and Frameworks* on page 153.

11   The Impact of World Wide Web Technology

You have already seen references in this book to information obtained from the World Wide Web on the Internet. For our purposes, we have to delve into why this particular brand of client/server technology is attracting so much attention and why it is rapidly becoming another value-adding information systems technology in large organizations.

While most of the public's attention has been focused on the World Wide Web on the Internet and the access that it provides to information and businesses, it is also possible to use Web technology in a more private setting. Many organizations are setting up Web servers that are only accessible internally or to specifically designated end-users. They can then provide information and applications that might not have been appropriate on the public network, even with improved security controls. Using Internet access protocols internally (i.e., creating an "Intranet") and Web technology to create client/server applications will be an important tool in IS's arsenal for at least the next several years.

11.1   WHAT ARE THE INTERNET AND THE WORLD WIDE WEB?

The Internet, a global "network of computer networks," has grown out of experiments with heterogeneous networking begun 25 years ago by the Advanced Research Projects Agency of the US Department of Defense. The intent was to provide a fail-safe capability for connecting disparate computers over large distances. The Internet today comprises millions of computers in most countries in the world (see Figure 19) inter-

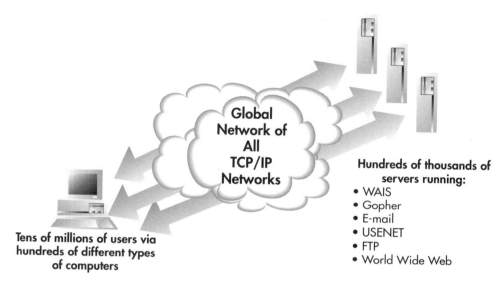

Figure 19: Client/server applications on the Internet

connected by millions of miles of telephone lines, fiber optic cables, and satellite links

The common connection protocol of the Internet is TCP/IP (Transmission Control Protocol/Internet Protocol), which controls the transmission and reception of packets of information. If you have a network in your organization capable of running the TCP/IP protocol, it can be connected to the Internet via one of the hundreds of Internet Service Providers that have sprung up over the past several years. ISPs include such diverse companies as AT&T and MCI (which also provide much of the cross-country backbone network of the Internet), PSINet and UUNET, and hundreds of small local providers. The portions of your TCP/IP network that are accessible only from within your organization (by limiting protocol routings) are sometimes referred to as an "Intranet."

The World Wide Web is one of many client/server applications that organizations make available over the Internet. Each Web site (specified by its "universal resource locator," i.e., address) is a server; each end-user referencing those sites with a Web "browser" is a client. The Web initially derived its value from integrating many of the other applications available on the Internet (carrying such names as FTP, Telnet, and Gopher) and making them easy to use. Before the creation of Web servers and browsers, getting access to the Internet and the contents available on connected machines was best left to your local UNIX guru. The introduction of inexpensive Web browsers (often given away free) changed that and was responsible for bringing the Internet to the typical PC user.

Using structured codes embedded in text files (called Hypertext Markup Language, HTML), anyone could develop highly sophisticated "Web pages." Web pages are files residing on Web servers that are transmitted to the client machine to execute. The embedded commands control formatting, hypertext links (to jump to other material), graphics, audio, and video. Some commands interact with the server to control the execution of server-based programs. Web pages (HTML files) quickly replaced simple text files as the primary content vehicle of the Internet.

For the information systems developer, the Web is proving to be a development environment that will make many kinds of client/server applications extremely easy to create. Web technology, including secure servers such as Netscape's Commerce Server and machine-independent programming languages such as Sun's Java, provide all that is needed to create downloadable applications with multimedia information (text, graphics, audio, and video) and secure data entry and inquiry—from anywhere in the world. As Figure 20 shows, gateways to existing applications permit Web technology to bring a wide range of internal systems directly to the Web browser on the desktop. As noted earlier, Web technology is enabling three-tier client/server applications with relatively "skinny" client machines, a highly cost-effective approach for many organizations.[16]

While additional software was needed to use the Web under Windows, Windows 95, OS/2, and many versions of UNIX now include browsers with the base operating systems. Proprietary on-line services such as America Online, Prodigy, and Compuserve also provide browsers as part of their readily available

---

16. See Section 7.3 *Fat Clients, Skinny Clients* on page 53.

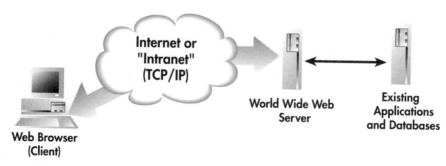

Figure 20: World Wide Web technology

software.[17] There are also plans to provide Internet and Web access via attachments to television and game sets. What this means is that almost everybody, both at his business and in his home, is going to have a Web browser on his desktops over the next few years, making Web-based client/server applications more accessible than any other kind ever invented.

There are numerous sources of information about the World Wide Web and Web technology, many available in your local book store and many others on-line—on the Web, of course. Try going to the original source for starters: http://www.ncsa.uiuc.edu (the Web site of the National Center for Supercomputer Applications), although almost every software and hardware manufacturer's Web site will provide you with some information and pointers to even more.

11.2   How the Internet and Web Technology Create Value

As Web technology becomes more pervasive, many organizations are rethinking their use of other, more complex client/server technologies. As access to the Internet becomes more pervasive, many organizations are rethinking the way in which they provide services to their customers—and even which services they provide. The relative advantages that Internet and

---

17. In May 1996, Compuserve announced that it was moving its proprietary information to the Internet, thus signaling the beginning of the end for proprietary on-line services running over proprietary networks. The future is proprietary services over the Internet.

Web technology bring to the client/server arena are literally remaking technology and business decisions all over the world.

Some of the earliest Web applications have already shown their value to market leading organizations. Federal Express[18] connected its mainframe-based package-tracking system to a Web server and made it possible for everyone to check on where his packages were at any time. In doing this, FedEx not only provided another channel for customer service but also provided it at extremely low per-transaction cost. Banks and securities firms are also integrating existing customer information systems with Web servers, as are other types of organizations that have customer accounts (universities, utilities, mail order houses, even government agencies). They are seeking the dual benefits of improving customer service (by providing another access mechanism to service) and reducing cost (by taking the human out of the loop for many types of transactions). It is rapidly becoming the norm for systems to include direct customer access via Web technology.

Many types of services can be brought to customers via the Internet and the Web. These range from simple information access to more sophisticated "user-controlled" information retrieval to even more sophisticated transaction processing, such as account maintenance and financial transactions. However, there seems to be a direct correlation between the value of the service being offered and the complexity of implementing that service, as Figure 21 shows.[19]

Web technology can be used to provide on-line access to static information such as corporate marketing brochures rather easily. Many of the first external Web sites provided little more than on-line versions of existing corporate documents (albeit with some hypertext links). It wasn't too long before organizations started including access to third-party "search engines" on their Web pages so that customers and other browsers would have even easier access to the specific information they were

---

18. Why does that name keep coming up?

19. Judy Cohen and Mark Raiffa have been working with me to study these different types of Web-based applications.

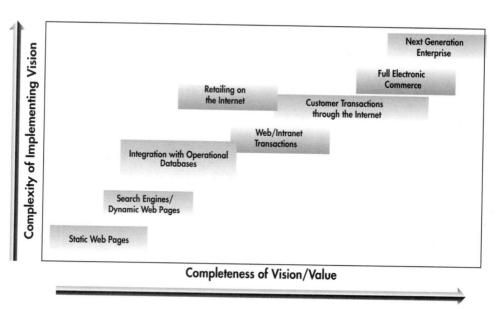

Figure 21: Internet/Web value model

looking for. After selecting search criteria, programs on the Web server would create an HTML page dynamically and sent that down to the end-user's browser. This approach allowed corporations to put such voluminous documents as parts catalogs and detailed product specifications "on the Web" without their customers feeling that they were lost in the stacks of some virtual library. All customers need to know is the address of a particular corporation's main or "home" page, and can work from there.[20]

These relatively-easy-to-implement Web applications clearly provided value to their organizations. For example, Digital Equipment Corporation was reported to have sold millions of dollars of their Alpha processors this way, much to their initial surprise. These applications, however, are just scratching the

---

20. And, of course, some of those same search engines have been applied across the thousands of Web servers and pages on the Internet to produce global indices. Several companies have been formed to provide this type of service, showing that the Web is fostering the creation of totally new service companies (some of which have gone public at amazing price/earnings multiples) as well as expanding the horizons of existing organizations.

surface of what is possible. Corporations, governments, and other non-profits alike wanted to move up the scale to use the Web for transaction processing, i.e., updating strategic databases under repeatable conditions. Accessing account balances wasn't enough (although even that required a level of security unknown to Internet aficionados of years past): customers should be allowed to input and update information as well. What these early adopters found was that, although the value was great, this was much more difficult to implement—in fact, almost as difficult as it would be using any other approach to client/server technology.

Although Web technology provides benefits of cross-platform execution (what is developed for one environment will work in all) and server-based storage of programs and data (thus avoiding the replication update problem), it is (in 1996) an immature technology with no history of implementing secure, reliable transaction-processing systems. Not wanting to be left behind in the rush to bring new services to their customers many corporations have moved ahead with home-grown solutions. We can expect many of these systems to be replaced by commercial products over the next couple of years, but they will have served their purpose: they will have brought their developers early value from the Internet and Web.

The highest level of value is created when organizations are totally "Web enabled": when the Internet, representing universal connectivity, and Web technology, representing a standardized approach to systems development, would provide new information systems technology rich enough to allow a rethinking of fundamental strategies and approaches to business. What would your organization be like if you knew that all your customers and potential customers, all your suppliers and potential suppliers, all your employees and potential employees were linked electronically with compatible and interoperable software? If you were a bank, would you have any branches? If you were a telecommunications company, what would your products be? If you were Federal Express, what would be your primary services—and to whom would you be sending your electronic bills? Completely rethinking an organization's role in the context of the new information systems technology will be necessary to ensure the survival of the enterprise into the twenty-first century. And many universities, corporations, and foundations are actively engaged in this pursuit today.

The Internet has turned into a tornado, swirling at incredibly high speeds, picking up everything in its path. It is fascinating to watch and even more fascinating to be in the middle of. It is truly a new information systems technology that is creating value—incredible amounts of value—for the organizations that can harness it.

12 Risks of Client/Server Implementation

Implementing client/server technology is not a "sure thing." That is, you cannot simply say to your information systems staff, "go implement client/server" and have them come back with a detailed schedule and task plan with a close-to-100 percent chance of being met. Why? And why is client/server a riskier undertaking than previous technologies before it?

I am sure that few in our field would argue that, even after 30 years experience implementing mainframe systems, we could always guarantee on-time delivery. But most would also agree that implementing mainframe systems is inherently less risky than implementing client/server systems. Here's why

- *Client/server is a "newer" technology.*

Client/server first entered the realm of management information systems in the mid-1980s. In ten or so years, we have implemented a large number of systems, but there are many aspects of client/server implementation that are hardly routine. In fact, it is more likely than not that the next client/server system you implement will involve some combination of hardware, software, and network components that no one has ever tried before!

- *The tools available to assist in implementation are fewer in number and less comprehensive than for mainframe technology.*

This is a direct consequence of the immaturity of the technology: software vendors need time to understand what the market needs are, to imple-

CHAPTER *12* *Risks of Client/Server Implementation*

ment new tools, and then to bring them to market. The 1990s have seen the introduction of literally hundreds of tools to assist in client/server implementation, but few have achieved the status and support that come with broad market acceptance.

- *Client/server architecture, involving as it does multiple computers and networks, is more difficult to analyze than mainframe application architecture.*

This is unlikely to change over time, although again the tools will get better.

- *Systems integration of multiple components from multiple vendors running on multiple machines is more complex.*

Bringing together multiple components from multiple software and hardware vendors is getting easier, but is still fraught with problems of incompatibilities. This is a particularly worrisome problem: while the situation is improving, there are structural factors that indicate that it will never go away.[21]

- *Performance issues are more difficult to pin down and correct.*

As a result of the more complex architecture, it is significantly more difficult to understand the impact that changes (often minor) in individual components will have. Performance modeling and simulation takes on a more important role in analyzing client/server systems than it has taken in the mainframe arena.

- *The functions and features of client/server systems seem to be harder to pin down.*

This is a somewhat artificial problem, but a real risk nonetheless. Given the number of enhancements and changes that we are constantly making to systems, it isn't clear that we have even been able to pin down exactly what it is that the end-users want and need. Another interpretation is that their wants and needs change with the introduction of the system. With the increased flexibility that client/server technology affords, it is possible to make more changes more rapidly, and that sometimes results in

---

21. See Section 10.1 *Standards and the Myth of Open Systems* on page 67 and Chapter 16 *Proving the Technical Architecture* on page 107.

functions seeming to change all the time. Incremental and iterative development methodologies have been codified to deal with just these issues.[22]

All of these issues spring from inherent characteristics of client/server technology in today's environment. Some of them will be solved (or at least reduced in impact) over time. Others, may not. And in any case, new risk factors will be introduced as the technology changes over time. For these reasons, risk management is itself an important activity in client/server implementation—and worthy of its own section later in this book.[23]

 CONNECTIONS: *Client/Server, Architecture, Components, Iterative Development, Risk Management*

The risks involved in client/server implementation presage the main topics in this book: architecture, component construction, iterative development, and management. Creating value with new technology requires an understanding of how to deal with the issues in implementing it successfully.

---

22. See *Iterative and Incremental Development* on page 197.

23. See Chapter 40 *Risk: Since You Can't Avoid It, Manage It* on page 251.

Architecture Is the Answer; What Is the Question?

Today's strategic applications are of a size and complexity that make them far too difficult to just "write the programs." First, we must have a plan that lays out the various components of the system and how they fit together. Even as the basic "design-code-test" cycle of common methodologies is being called into question, we find many of today's systems are too complex even to begin at this level and to require a higher level of analysis before design commences. This analysis is to create the "system architecture," so-named because of its analogy to the art and science of building architecture. Client/server systems, with their functions and data split over multiple computers, must be "architected" before we begin to design them, much less write their programs.

> ## Sentence first —verdict afterwards.[1]
>
> **Alice's Adventures in Wonderland**

---

1. In legal circles, this approach is frowned upon; in systems development projects, it is commonly applied.

In the system development life-cycle, the architectural stage is where we determine the overall structure of the system. It is where many key questions must be raised and addressed.

- How flexible should this system be, given changing business demands, that range from increasing or decreasing volume to the introduction or removal of major business functions?
- How flexible should this system be in the face of changing economics of technology?
- How flexible should this system be as it undergoes a variety of maintenance updates?
- How much of this system should we be able to complete with "off-the-shelf" components, both hardware and software?
- How much standardization and commonality should be built in, i.e., how much of the programming from one part of the system should be reused in another part of the system?
- How will we achieve the appropriate balance of flexibility, cost, performance, and usability, (plus other key factors) that have been identified with the success of the system?

Those are the questions; architecture, and in particular, applying accepted principles of good system architecture to creating the system, will allow us to create the answers. As we proceed through this discussion, however, keep in mind that "the system architecture" is not a single concept or even a static concept: it is the combination of many different views of the system at many points in time. That is what makes the architectural process so difficult—and so important.

13 Defining System Architecture

The architecture of a system is a comprehensive framework that describes its form and structure—its components and how they fit together (no distinction here between hardware and software since a system's architecture comprises both). A generic system architecture is an overall framework that describes the structure of a large number of systems, such as business systems or manufacturing systems. A specific system architecture is the framework that describes that particular system (it is that system's architecture).

In general, a complete architectural plan addresses the functions that the system provides, the hardware and network that are used to develop and operate it, and the software that is used to develop and operate it. Thesystem architecture is thus composed of the component architectures shown in Figure 22.

Functional architecture defines the breakdown of application function into systems, subsystems, and lower-level functional areas, depending on the level of detail addressed. This is sometimes called the *application architecture*. (Everything else is sometimes called the *technical architecture*.)

Hardware and network architecture shows the computers and networks involved in developing and processing the application.

Software architecture defines the components of and relationships among all the software involved in developing, testing, and operating the application. The software architecture includes operating systems, database management sys-

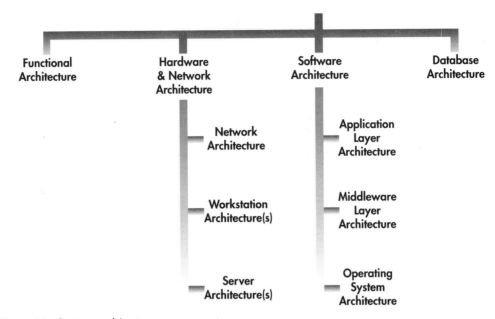

Figure 22: System architecture components

tems, middleware,[2] and other common modules, as well as the components of the application function itself. The software architecture used in the development environment is shown separately as is the software architecture used in the quality assurance and testing environment.

Database architecture defines databases, their relationships, where they reside (on the hardware and network architecture), and their structure. Different database architectures may be defined for the operational system, for development activities (which may have multiple copies of key databases), and for quality assurance and testing purposes.

The complete system architecture comprises more than these four breakouts, however. Each of these

---

2. See Section 22.1 *Middleware* on page 150.

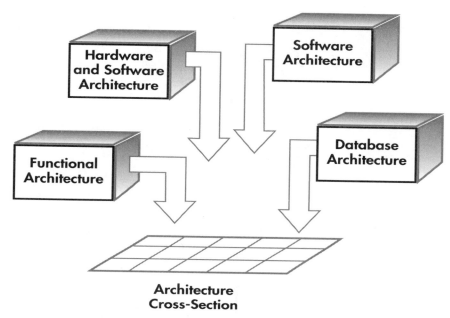

Figure 23: Dimensions of system architecture

components of system architecture can be thought of as representing a different dimension of the complete system architecture so that it is possible to view many different "cross-sections" (as depicted in Figure 23). For example, a complete understanding of a system architecture might involve the following cross-dimension diagrams:

- *Functions overlaid on hardware and network*: showing which functions are performed on which computers and where they are located in the network (see Figure 24).

- *Functions overlaid on software*: showing the components that implement different functional modules.

- *Software overlaid on hardware and network*: showing which software components execute on which computers.

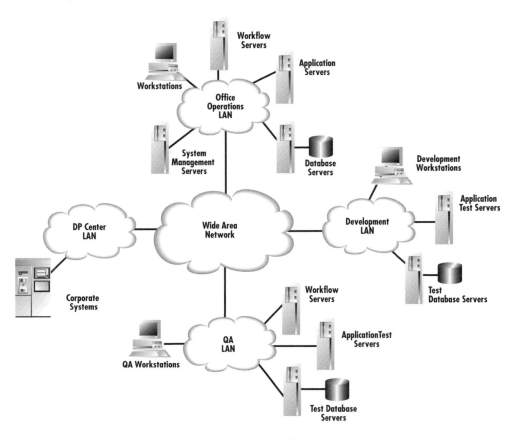

Figure 24: Functions overlaid on hardware and network architecture

- *Database overlaid on functions*: showing which databases are created and referenced by which functions.
- *Database overlaid on hardware and network*: showing which databases reside on which computers (see Figure 25).
- *Database overlaid on software*: showing which databases are created and referenced by which software components.

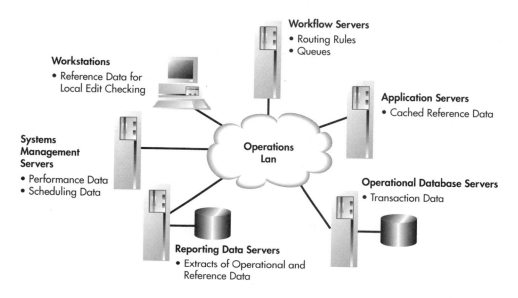

Figure 25: Database overlaid on hardware and network architecture

Each view of a system's architecture provides new insights into the capabilities of the system. Creating a complete system architecture is the process of taking a complex, four-dimensional problem and solving it by creating and analyzing a variety of two- and three-dimensional views. You won't necessarily need every possible view to solve the problem, but you might.

14 The Power of a Well "Architected" System

Material in this section is adapted from [Grochow 1992].

An article in *Information Week* had a rather startling statement:

> "NASD (National Association of Security Dealers) touts SMART's technology as forming the basis for 'the stock market for the next 100 years.'" [page 20, April 20, 1992, "NASDAQ Plans Global Conquest"]

It would appear that the NASDAQ expects to write systems that will last 100 years! Crazy? Probably not—particularly when you consider that they plan to spend $100 million doing it. If you were spending that much money, wouldn't you like to know that your investment had a fairly long life—why not 100 years?

Cars last 10 years (sometimes); refrigerators—20; houses—100; municipal buildings—hundreds. If architects can design buildings to last; computer system architects can design their systems to last, too. What it takes is knowing your objectives and constraints and adhering to good architectural principles.

As system developers, we already understand this to a certain degree. Some systems in use today are already over 20 years old and have several years of useful life left. Some systems have long since been replaced by this age. What is it about the long-lasting systems that has allowed their owners to keep them in productive service for so long? (We are, of course, discounting those systems that are running "unproductively" and should have been killed off long ago.)

Long-lasting computer systems have the same basic characteristic of other long-lasting systems:

their architects knew what they were doing, had a sense of style, and built them with an eye to maintainability and providing long-lasting value. Most of us probably know, at least intuitively, what this means in terms of a building, but in the case of computer systems it needs further explanation.

Computer systems need to be updated on a regular basis to meet the changing demands of the people and organizations using them. Adding pharmacies to its department stores requires a major retailer to add new systems features to their stock-keeping systems. The need to create new derivative securities requires almost constant modification to a wide range of systems in an investment banking firm. New government regulations force an oil company to make modifications in its partnership accounting system. And 100 percent annual growth in sales volume causes a major software company to do a major update to its order-processing and manufacturing systems.

The reasons that systems need to be modified or updated are never-ending, and a good systems architect will take this fact into account: long-lasting systems are built with flexibility in mind. The more flexible the architecture, the more the system can take in terms of updates and enhancements. Of course, flexibility of this type often is only one factor in designing a system, a factor that is sometimes traded off with other factors, such as cost and performance.

Everything needs maintenance. Owners of buildings that last hundreds of years have typically spent several times their initial investment in maintenance costs (repair and renovation). But it was still worth the effort (i.e., it was an economical thing to do), or they wouldn't have done it. We face the same types of decisions regarding computer systems: do we spend a certain amount on maintenance each year (thereby extending the useful life of the system), or do we throw out the system and start over? If the existing system (house or computer) is structurally sound, proper maintenance can keep it in top condition. If the underlying structure is flawed or too inflexible to be updated, maintenance will not be justified economically.

The way to maintainability is to ensure that changes in one area of a system have as small an effect as possible on other areas. If you want to add a graphic user interface, why should you have to change an interest calculation module? If you want to add a new function that requires new data, why should you have to change programs that don't use that new data? If you want to restructure the database to improve performance in one part of the system, why should you have to modify programs in another part that don't need that level of performance? And if you want to run part of the system on a separate computer, why should you have to restructure other parts of the system to allow this to happen?

 CONNECTIONS: *Architecture, Object Technology*

The answer to all these questions is that you don't—if you made modularity, isolation of function, and data independence your key design criteria. Systems architects have employed these criteria for many years in creating flexible "layered" application software. They are also the key criteria employed in creating object-oriented software. In both cases, each unit (layer or object) presents a standard interface so that only directly cooperating units are affected by changes in each other. Other layers or objects not involved with the ones that changed are not impacted.

It eventually boils down to economics. As a developer and consultant, I have been involved in many projects to determine the economics of developing new systems to replace old ones. We consider all the alternatives: staying with the current system, doing a partial replacement, using the latest "reengineering" technology, etc. The systems that are replaced meet that fate because they are not maintainable at a reasonable cost, and sometimes not at any cost!

So, we get to the final word on computer system longevity: if we act as architects in designing our systems, following principles related to appropriate use of materials (in our case, computer hardware, operating systems, languages and tools), modularity, maintainability, and structural integrity (i.e., good "system architecture"), we will end up with systems that are structurally sound. And systems that are structurally sound will last a long time. Perhaps even 100 years.

14.1 THE POWER OF AN ARCHITECTURAL OVERSIGHT: HOW TWO BYTES CAN COST BILLIONS

Many systems won't last 100 years—in fact, some aren't even going to last ten. In particular, one type of system is going to die in 1999, or at least give incorrect results when the calendar hits January 1, 2000. I refer to those systems that carry only two digits for the year in date fields and computations scattered through their code and databases. Most of those systems will fail because their designers didn't understand that well architected systems can have very long life times—life times that span century (or millennial) boundaries.[3]

We all know the problem: by the time you read this book, you will have already come up with a strategy for dealing with it in your organization. In some cases, you will have thrown out a system and replaced it with another. In other cases, you will have spent a very large sum on doing what is ultimately unproductive work: fixing a bug that was designed to cause problems. The Gartner Group has estimated that U.S. industry will spend $300–$600 billion fixing the Mil-

---

3. Many systems will hit the year 2000 before the calendar does. Life insurance systems have been printing out schedules to the year 2000 for at least 30 or 40 years. More and more systems will hit 2000 as we get closer and closer. Some of yours probably already have.

lennium Bug, and that half of all organizations will still have some system fail when it hits (see [Terdiman 1996]).

The architectural issue is straightforward: systems were designed with the idea that they would be replaced before too many years had elapsed. What started off as a legitimate attempt to save on costly memory and storage (it was costly in 1970 and 1980) turned into an absolute nightmare. If we had been architects taking the long view, we could still have saved that storage space without creating future chaos (although at the cost of some additional computations—everything is a trade-off). All it would have taken is for someone on the project team to have said, "But what if our system is still in operation 20 years from now, or 25, or 30?" and stuck to his or her guns when everyone laughed.

So, now that we're past that issue, on to the next date-related challenge: is 2000 a leap year, and what about 2100?[4]

---

4. Believe it or not, some IS folks still aren't sure (there was actually a "debate" about this in the letters column of a popular trade magazine). Years divisible by 4 are leap-years, except for years divisible by 100—unless that year is also divisible by 400. 2000 is; 2100 isn't. Pope Gregory XIII really had some long-range thinkers on his staff. We'll be OK until approximately the year 4000, when minor differences will start to add up again.

15 The Logical-Physical Spectrum

IS professionals are always talking about the "logical" view of something versus the "physical" view, particularly when discussing different components of system architecture. In the case of architecture, a logical view is a generic "model" or diagram of system components and how they fit together, shown without regard to specific "physical" software, hardware, or network components. For example, a logical view of the database architecture might show a "customer database," but would not specify what database management system it was to be implemented in or even the particular computer it was to reside on. A physical view overlays some or all of those specifics of hardware, software, and network.

In practice, you will often see some logical components superimposed on some physical components and vice versa. You might see a "customer database" (without further physical specification) residing on a dual-Pentium computer as a database server, or you might see a Sybase-SQL Server customer database residing on an unspecified machine. In fact, you can create a wide variety of logical and physical diagrams, ranging from a "generic" logical diagram (with absolutely no indication of physical constraints) to a "specific" physical diagram (showing the exact hardware and software components right down to the version number) as Figure 26 indicates. During the process of developing client/server systems, you will need several types of diagrams along the logical-physical or generic-specific spectrum.[5]

---

5. I am indebted to Linda Gilpin for her suggestions on this taxonomy.

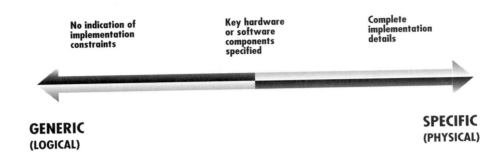

Figure 26: Logical-physical architecture continuum

CONNECTIONS: *Client/Server Architecture*

Particularly in the case of client/server systems, it is important to consider the full range of logical (generic) and physical (specific) architecture views throughout the system life-cycle. It is not simply the case that you work first with the logical architecture and then with the physical one. In general, the logical architecture determines what physical architectures will be feasible. However, physical hardware or software constraints will make some of those physical architectures infeasible. Therefore, the logical architecture may need to be reconsidered during discussions of physical architecture.[6]

---

6. It is interesting to note that hardware and software manufacturers often introduce the most constraints into the design of the system architecture. "This database will work only on that hardware" or "That function library requires this operating system" are among the most common type of issues that systems architects have to deal with. Unfortunately, they are often somewhat more subtle, e.g. ,"Release 1.4.3 of the database requires release 3.1.1a of the operating system, that unfortunately isn't supported by release 1.0 of the function library." Many system delays can be attributed to the sudden realization of these kinds of incompatibility chains. See Chapter 16 *Proving the Technical Architecture* on page 107 for further discussion.

For example, a system logical architecture might portray a single large database. Discussions of physical constraints such as response time from a database server might require that the database be subdivided among different servers. You might then wish to portray an architecture diagram showing the multiple database servers (i.e., adding a physical constraint), but without indicating a specific type of database management system or hardware (i.e., keeping these at the "logical" level).

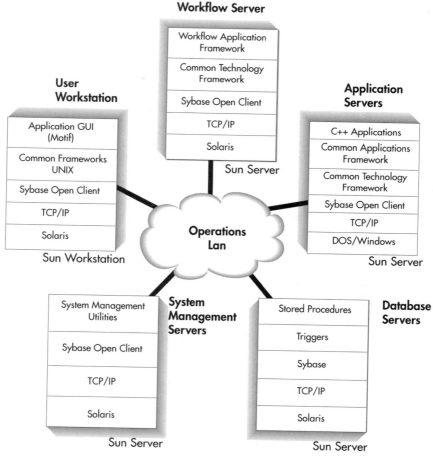

Figure 27: Example hybrid logical-physical system architecture

Figure 27 is an example of a system architecture diagram showing physical hardware and physical software but a logical network (it does not show the exact number of computers, their exact placement on local and wide area networks, or any of the details of the network infrastructure). It is one of the kinds of logical-physical diagrams that architects, designers, programmers, and implementers of client/server system find useful in describing their plans.

15.1   SYSTEM "LOGICAL" ARCHITECTURE

One way of describing the logical architecture of a system is as a series of layers and tiers, each identifying a class of system functions. Figure 28 shows one possible approach, an architecture with five major layers and tiers, where the relative positions indicate functions that communicate with each other and those that are isolated from each other. For example, all parts of the system can communicate with the operating system, but only the application "business functions" communicates with the database access component.

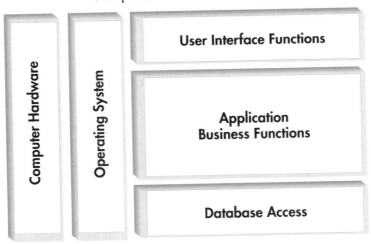

Figure 28: System logical architecture

Although all layers are obviously using the computer hardware, it is shown vertically next to the operating system to indicate that it is the operating system's job to isolate the rest of the system from the specifics of the hardware configuration. This approach is common to modern operating systems and to the extent that it is done well, allows portability of applications among different types of hardware.[7]

CONNECTIONS: *Client/Server Architecture*

Take off the operating system and hardware levels and you have the "three tier" (or three level) client/server architecture that we talked about. While this is often used as a starting point in talking about client/server architecture, it does not go nearly far enough in explaining how the system is put together—even from a logical viewpoint.

The next logical view that is fairly popular begins to show some of the structure of the system components. In Figure 29, the second level, application business functions, has been divided into several parallel tiers indicating the presence of functions of a similar type. In a corporate accounting system for example, these tiers might be labeled General Ledger, Accounts Payable, Accounts Receivable, and Billing.

The application function level is what might be thought of as the heart of the application system. Each tier consists of those programs that provide a certain set of functions to the user (via the user interface) and that call upon services from the next lower level, in this diagram the database access level. You can use this type of diagram (with more specific labeling) to depict the overall logical structure of an entire

---

7. It is also one aspect of the "open systems" approach discussed in Chapter 10 *What Do We Mean by Open Systems?* on page 65.

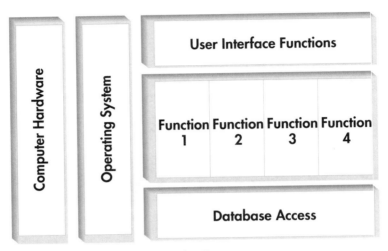

Figure 29: System logical architecture beginning detail

system, or just the logical structure found on a specific computer in the client/server network.

In Figure 30, the application function level is split into a level showing the major functions (as parallel tiers) and a level of common business functions. Common business functions are those facilities commonly needed by many applications in a particular functional area. The contents of this tier are typically specific to a particular domain (e.g., accounting or banking). This diagram shows one way of further splitting the application business functions into components, by separating out common functions to be used across all areas of the system. (Don't be too confused by the fact that the function layer names are the same even though the level represents different software in the two diagrams. Naming is not standardized in these types of architectural diagrams and context is important.)

In the financial services industry, many different systems need to associate a customer number with the different account numbers assigned to that customer for various loans and deposit accounts. A pro-

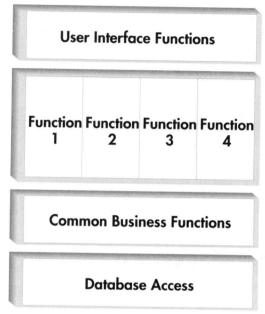

Figure 30: More detailed layered architecture

gram to perform the required database accesses and validations might become part of a common business functions tier for financial industry systems. In the oil industry, a similar requirement might be to find the wells and properties owned by a particular individual. In the telecommunications industry, it might be to find a person's multiple telephone numbers. Each function is common to the systems in its domain, but not to the others.

Cross-functional area services such as security control, transaction error processing, report production, and many others can be contrasted with the previously described functional area services. These services might be shown in yet another layer breaking out common application services. Software in this layer could be used in a wider variety of application systems without regard to the functional area. Even here, different common application services might be needed for significantly different applications, such as transaction processing applications versus decision support.

As you study application systems in more detail, you realize that it is very difficult to program a system with completely isolated tiers. More practically, isolation is seen as a goal rather than an absolute requirement. Some designers show architecture diagrams with a series of stair steps (as in Figure 31) to indicate that the business function specific programs may need access to each of the lower levels. (The operating system level in this diagram is split into a level showing major middleware functions and a level showing the base operating system. In addition, the operating system is shown in this diagram as a horizontal level, indicating that it is the further job of the middleware to isolate the remainder of the application system from the operating system—architectural diagrams can contain many subtleties.)

CONNECTIONS: *Architecture and Components*

Figure 30 and Figure 31 show application systems that reuse common parts or components. Viewing each program in a system as a constituent part of a particular architectural layer serves to isolate programs in one layer from changes in the others. A significant result of this view is to simplify design and maintenance of applications by encouraging the reuse of entire layers or tiers of software.

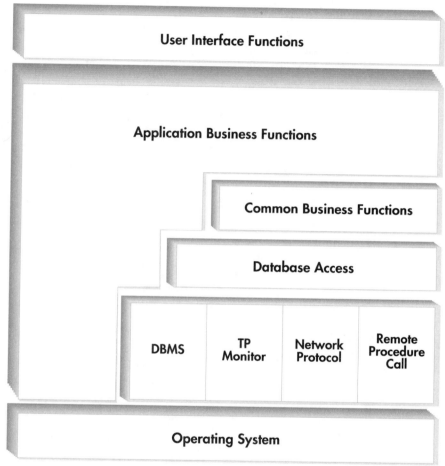

Figure 31: Stair-stepped application architecture

15.2 SYSTEM MANAGEMENT ARCHITECTURE

Another aspect of the system that often requires its own architectural diagram is system management. System management refers to functions such as network administration, configuration management, performance monitoring, problem reporting, accounting, production control, and software distribution.

An architectural diagram would show major system management processes and where they are performed, e.g. separate servers for backup, modules on each server for performance data collection. Figure 32 is an example.]

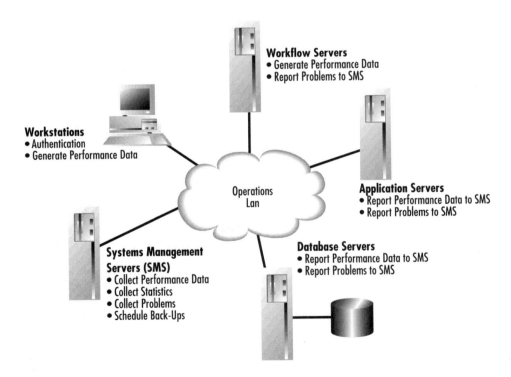

Figure 32: System management architecture

15.3   ARCHITECTURE FOR DIFFERENT PHASES OF THE PROJECT

So far, we have been tacitly assuming that the architecture discussion centered around the operational or production system. However, the architecture of the development and testing environments used to create that system also have to be designed and developed.[8]

Figure 33 shows a logical software development architecture overlaid on a logical hardware architecture for the development of a major system.[9] Figure 34 shows the arrangement of databases used by the developers. You can see that they show a different architecture than would be found in the operational environment.

As a project progresses from initial development to testing and then operation, the project team will need to adjust its development environment. Once a system goes into production, the team will still need an environment for developing and testing changes. From the development environment, software will move into the quality assurance environment, from there into production, and then back into development for modification and enhancement (as shown in Figure 35).

---

8. Another of the major causes of client/server system development delays and cost overruns is failure to allow for the creation and maintenance of these environments. I recall being in a project review not too long ago where the manager in charge presented his estimates for creating the development environment. He proudly stated that this was the same estimate they had used on two previous similar projects, although those projects had overrun this task by 200 percent and 100 percent respectively. This time they would hit it right on the button. I suggested that there was an equally likely possibility that this time they would go back to overrunning by 200 percent since the only thing his numbers showed was that they had no idea what the right estimate was. "Hope springs eternal..."

9. Actually, you might call these "semi-physical" (which I like better than "semi-logical") since some components are specified in concrete terms.

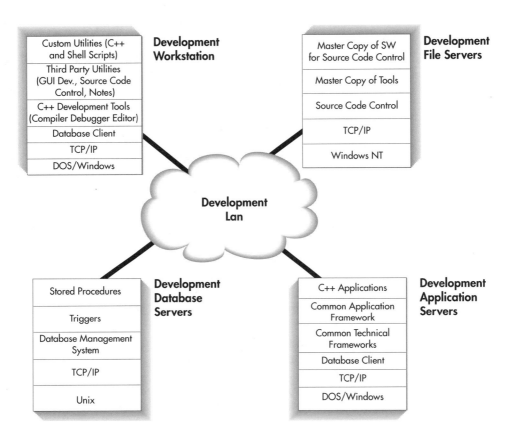

Figure 33: Software development environment overlaid on hardware architecture

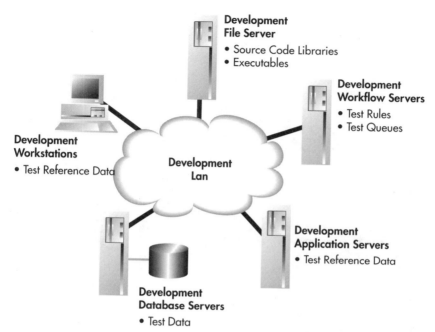

Development File Server
- Source Code Libraries
- Executables

Development Workflow Servers
- Test Rules
- Test Queues

Development Workstations
- Test Reference Data

Development Lan

Development Database Servers
- Test Data

Development Application Servers
- Test Reference Data

Figure 34: Development database architecture

The bottom line of this discussion is that *the* system architecture is not a single concept or even a static concept: it is the combination of many different views of the system at many points in time. Deciding which are most important in developing any specific system, which are going to best illuminate the potential problems, which are going to make it clear to the designers and developers what they are going to have to do to implement the system, is the most important task for the system architect.

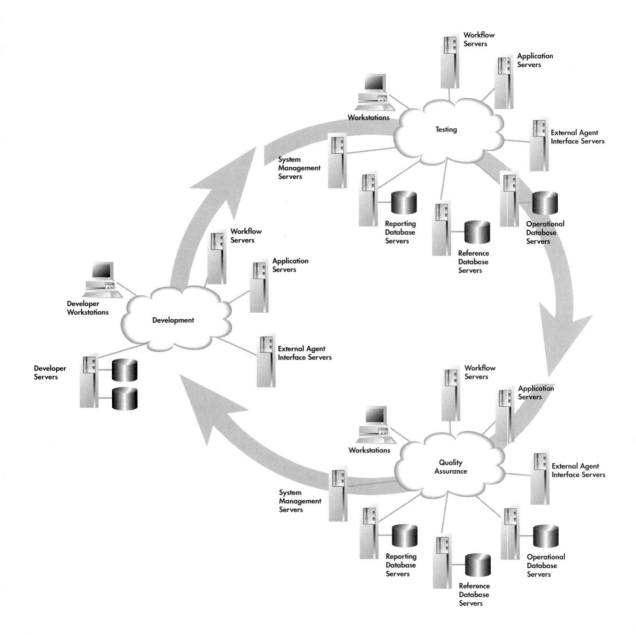

Figure 35: Development database architecture through the life-cycle

16 Proving the Technical Architecture

> *There's no use trying,* Alice said: *one can't believe impossible things.*
>
> *I daresay you haven't had much practice,* said the Queen. *When I was your age, I always did it for half-an-hour a day. Why, sometimes I've believed as many as six impossible things before breakfast.*
>
> Through the Looking Glass

Given the absence of truly open systems, prudent developers will verify that the set of hardware and software products they are planning to use really work together as expected. It is not necessarily impossible that they will, but you must go through the process of "proving the technical architecture" to corroborate vendor claims. Does the particular version of the database management system work on the server hardware you have, using the network protocol in your network, to connect to the workstation a typical user will use, with all the software that a typical user will have? At best, this is a non-trivial question; at worst, a months-long project in itself.

Because of the uncertainties associated with proving the technical architecture, this step in the life-cycle has to be performed in parallel with design of the application. It should be started as soon as the major hardware and software components have been specified. The technical proof of concept may show that some of those products have to be reevaluated and substitutions made to create an acceptable client/server architecture. Anyone who waits until the application code is about to go into testing before proving viability of the technical architecture is asking for trouble.

Proving the technical architecture means that you have to assemble a prototypical environment, all the way from a developer's workstation to the application and database servers to the end-user's workstation. Seemingly trivial differences between the prototyping environment and operational environment could mean significantly different results (see below). Not only do you need the same-brand software packages that you expect to use in development and operation, but all the same releases and version numbers. A combination that works may not work with a different version of just one product.

CONNECTIONS: *Client/Server Architecture vs. Components*

The architecture of a client/server system isn't complete until the specific hardware and software components have been tested together. All those technical architecture diagrams your team has been drawing only represent ideas until they have been shown to work in real life. An unfortunate fact about the new information systems technology is that what should work doesn't always. One of the downsides of the component approach is that sometimes those components are incompatible.

16.1 AND PROVING IT AGAIN...AND AGAIN

What is so interesting about technical prototyping of client/server systems: the task seems never to be finished. The reason can be traced back to the basic concept of client/server systems as constructed from interconnected components.

Let's say that you have software products in your system from a dozen or so vendors:

• a desktop operating system

- a server operating system (maybe from the same vendor, maybe not)
- a database manager (e.g., Sybase, Oracle, Informix)
- a development tool with run-time components (e.g., Powerbuilder, SQL Windows, Visual Basic, Open Interface, Galaxy)
- one or more subroutine or class libraries (lots of these since they reduce the amount of code you have to write to handle common functions)
- one or more network drivers (e.g., TCP/IP, Netbios, SPX/IPX)
- a language compiler (e.g., C, C + + , Smalltalk)
- an inquiry or reporting package
- packaged applications
- productivity tools (e.g., spreadsheets, word processors, calendars, CAD)
- electronic mail

Each of your vendors can usually be counted on to release a new version of its software at least once a year, some even more often if they find bugs or other deficiencies that need correcting. With twelve vendors, this means that on average you can expect one new release of something every month. This means that your project team will see enough new software over the course of the development to drive everyone crazy—if they attempt to deal with it all.

And, of course, that is the key: you can't deal with it all. Somewhere along the way, you have to say "enough is enough" and go with the configuration of software releases that you have currently tested and working. At least, that's what you would like to do. Unfortunately, the interactions among programs and the "cascading release syndrome" will get you every time: a problem is fixed by a new release of software product A that is incompatible with the release of software product B that you are using or that requires the installation of a new release of software product C that you would rather not tackle at this time. It can drive you nuts...

16.2 DEALING EFFECTIVELY WITH UPGRADES AND NEW RELEASES

Proving the technical architecture is dealing with one part of the systems integration problem: ensuring that selected releases of selected components work together. Another part of the problem is selecting the releases in the first place and having a policy for dealing with new releases that appear during the course of development. Just as it is impossible to say that the design is frozen, it is impossible to say that the hardware and software configuration is frozen (as shown in the scenario just described). But you can establish some rules.

First, you must make it clear that any change in software, no matter how seemingly trivial, must be logged and tested. Those extra letters or numbers after the major release number signal that some of the code has been changed, perhaps in an area that will affect its integration with other components. You don't really know how much has been changed in version 3.0c1 over version 3.0c, let alone version 3.0. Even if the vendor lists the changes, it is almost impossible to ensure that no other areas have been impacted—or that those changes will not have unintended consequences themselves.

It helps to have an on-going relationship with your vendors, at least the key ones, so that you'll be notified of the availability of new releases of their products.[10] Minor releases are not generally advertised to the general public, but they are often made available to organizations in one of the vendor's third-party

---

10. At AMS, we have more than 100 such relationships and use a Notes database application to track interactions with vendors and suppliers occurring in different parts of the company. While few organizations other than systems integrators will have this many relationships, several dozen is not unusual.

relationship programs. Such programs go under such names as Systems Integrator, Solution Provider, Solution Partner. It doesn't matter what program you are in as long as you have access to the latest technical support and release information.

You should assume instability and change in your hardware and software environment. No matter how hard you try, you will be unable to ensure that all users have exactly the same hardware and software configurations (something as seemingly standard as a computer monitor has been known to trip up the unsuspecting integration team). This means that systems integration becomes a full-time activity, both for a project team and for an IS department. Creating a systems integration services group in your IS organization will save several times its cost in reduced time and effort for your project teams, as well as a much decreased frustration factor.

Ultimately, you will be faced with a decision about incorporating a new version of some product into your system just at the wrong time. There is no hard and fast rule for when and why to do this, but you are strongly encouraged to err on the side of caution. Presumably, the new version is being suggested to solve some problem that has surfaced late in the system development project. If there is any other way to solve your problem, including applying temporary patches, take it. You can never be sure that the new version of the product in question won't introduce more problems than it solves.

The component approach to development brings many advantages and potential cost savings. As I have noted before, however, in our "non-standard open systems" world, ease of component integration isn't one of them. And that takes us to the next topic...

What Is an *Object* Anyway?

Regardless of whether you subscribe to the view that objects will take over the world or that object technology is bound to be replaced by something easier to understand, you would have to agree that the term "object-oriented" has entered the common vocabulary of computing. Usually appearing as an adjective (as in object-oriented design, object-oriented programming, object-oriented system, etc.), the term is applied to everything from specific analytical techniques to development tools to applications. To understand all these, we have to first understand the new information systems technology definition of the root of it all, the "object."

Object technology got its start some 25 years ago when developers of simulation systems began architecting their systems in terms of the real-world objects making up those real-world

> **When I use a word,** Humpty Dumpty said in a rather scornful tone, *it means just what I choose it to mean—neither more nor less.*
>
> *Through the Looking Glass*

systems. If they were modeling the cruise control system in an automobile (a classic example), then the objects included the accelerator, the controls, the throttle, and the brakes. The recognition that most systems, including business systems, were actually modeling real-world systems led to the broader use of object-oriented analysis as a technique and objects as building blocks to be used in general computer systems development.

An "object" is a programming model of a real-world object. Viewed from the outside-in, the object is a model, but viewed from the inside-out, an object is a programming unit that contains program code and "working storage" data. By hiding the internal structure of the programs and the data, and by requiring all access via public "methods" (programming interfaces), developing programming objects forces a much higher degree of modularity than any other programming style. Modular programming with encapsulated objects "layers" the total complexity of systems by hiding complexity within objects (that successively reference objects that reference objects). This technique of layering complexity (which is also what we do by buying components and including them as parts of larger systems) is what allows us to develop increasingly large and functionally rich systems. It is the technique that allows us to develop the systems that end-users are demanding.

17 A Brief Tutorial on Object Orientation

"Objects" are:

- abstractions of real-world things,
- combinations of program code and data,
- another way of thinking about the basic building blocks of computer software.

In user terms, typical objects might be pictures on a screen representing documents, files, accounting transactions, purchase orders (as depicted in Figure 36), mail boxes, or telephones. In programming terms, objects are combinations of data structures and procedures that perform certain functions on that data. And in architectural terms, objects are a different way of thinking about the components of a software system.

Object-oriented analysis, design, and programming deal with the development of systems based on "objects" as the basic building blocks, rather than on the data structures or procedures individually. Object-oriented systems contain data structures and procedures, as do all systems, but it is the objects that are the fundamental focus.

Just as quantum physics is based on a wave-particle duality, you can view objects as

- components in a hierarchically arranged structure constituting a system, or
- self-contained software modules floating around in "object space" waiting for messages from other objects telling them to do some work.

Contrast this with the traditional single view of a system as a hierarchically structured set of pro-

Purchase Order   # Purchase Order Object

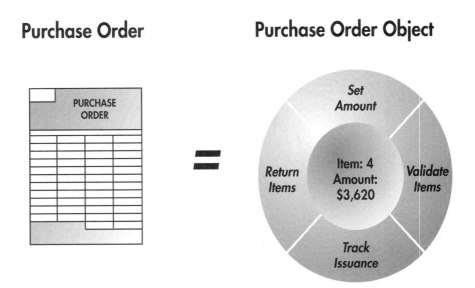

Figure 36: An object

grams, each performing its work in turn as the system proceeds from start to finish. It is this second view of object systems, as systems comprising independent units that communicate via messages, that distinguishes the object-oriented programming approach from more traditional ones.[1]

Many object text books begin with a statement such as began this section: "Objects are abstractions of real-world things; they are models of the behavior of these things in the real world." One of the dirty little secrets of the object community is that not all objects represent real world things. In fact, typical application systems have as many or more "technical" objects as "real-world" objects. For example, in [Gamma 1995], almost all of the design patterns are for creating objects that have nothing to do

---

1. Those who is old enough to have done I/O controller programming in his past or who have implemented the lowest-level interrupt routines in an operating system will note the similarity between this approach and the "self-contained routine sitting waiting for an interrupt" that they programmed in these other situations. With objects, however, message passing and interrupts occur at the level of the application and the user interface rather than just at the lowest levels of communicating with the hardware.

with the real-world of the application, but everything to do with techniques for implementing them efficiently given the state of today's object-programming environments. Although objects such as "proxies," "mediators," and "visitors" allow programmers to make their object programs more modular and generic and hence more flexible, they are a far cry from "customer," "invoice," and "product" objects that are the real world of the application.

The key to understanding why the object approach is important, however, is not to begin at the object level or to try to understand each object class in a system. Rather, it is to focus on the role of object principles in enforcing in practice the concepts of modularity and separability of function that will allow us to develop more powerful and flexible systems.

17.1 FORMAL DEFINITION

An "object" is the combination of a set of procedures and the data on which they operate that behaves in certain defined ways based on its inputs ("messages") and its heritage ("object class").

The functions an object's procedures perform are called "methods."

An "object class" (also called "object type") defines objects having some similar methods and attributes.

An "instance" of an object class is an object with specified values for its data attributes.

Object orientation is further defined by the properties that objects have. These properties are:

- abstraction
- encapsulation
- modularity (information hiding)
- hierarchical inheritance.

The data in an object represent abstract data types. An abstract data type is a data structure defined for the commonality of the operations performed on it. An "accounts payable voucher" is an abstract data type; a "four character string" is not. An instance of an abstract data type can be looked at and manipulated only by the common operations that are defined on it.

Thus, the data in an object are "encapsulated" by the procedures of the object (called "methods"); i.e., the procedures provide the only way in which the data can be accessed and manipulated. Procedures that are outside of a particular object can access that object's data only via the methods contained in that object.

Object methods have the property of "information hiding." Their defined interfaces reveal as little as possible about how they are implemented. In effect, each type of object (object class) becomes a new meta-instruction to the computer. We can use that meta-instruction quite effectively without delving any deeper into its inner workings.

Objects have the property of inheritance. They inherit data attributes and methods from other objects in the object class to which they are hierarchically related. "Accounts payable vouchers" inherit many attributes and methods from the "accounts payable transactions" class, which in turn inherits from the "accounting transaction" class.

Other properties have been included in some definitions of object orientation.

- Objects communicate with each other via "messages." Objects may, therefore, operate asynchronously or synchronously.
- Object classes should have the property of "multiple inheritance" through multiple levels and paths in a class hierarchy.
- Many object classes should be able to use the same messaging protocol, although the underlying method implementation will vary from class to class. This property is called "polymorphism." It allows the design of general purpose algorithms that can be applied to many different types of data (object instances).
- Objects are composed of other objects. Such a "composite" object contains these other objects directly rather than "inheriting" their properties.

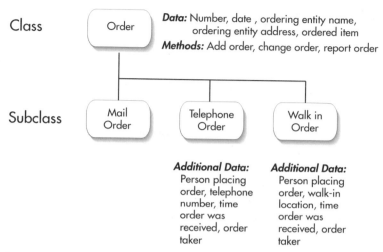

Figure 37: Object inheritance

- Object-oriented systems are constructed from objects contained in object libraries. Many of the objects in an object library should be reusable across multiple systems.

Applying these definitions, an object-oriented system appears in many ways similar to any structured, modular system. After all, a well-designed modular system can be expected to employ techniques such as encapsulation and information hiding, two key properties attributed to object-oriented systems.

Many of these properties can be illustrated in a simple example of part of a system to process orders for a retailer. If the designer defines an "order" *object class*, then "mail order," "telephone order," and "walk-in order" would all be members of the object class "order" (as Figure 37 shows).[2] The data structure associated with a generic order would form the core of the data structure of specific types of orders. *Methods* to add orders, change orders, and report various order information could be implemented as part of the order object. Only the additional

---

2. The "order" object in this case will never exist in a real system because all actual orders are either mail orders, walk-in orders, or telephone orders. The order object thus becomes a placeholder or what is know as an "abstract class."

attributes of a telephone order (e.g., the telephone number of the caller and the time of the call) or a walk-in order (the walk-in location) need be added to the generic attributes of an order.

Figure 38 illustrates *encapsulation* and *inheritance*. In this example, a bill object needs to know ordering information in order to produce a bill. Since methods encapsulate the data in objects, the only way to access data is by sending a message requesting that data. The bill object sends a message to the telephone order object. Since the report order method is inherited from the object class, the code in the order object is executed. Both the data definitions and all methods in the order class will be automatically available to all types of orders, because these subclass objects have access to this information via the inheritance mechanism of the object environment.

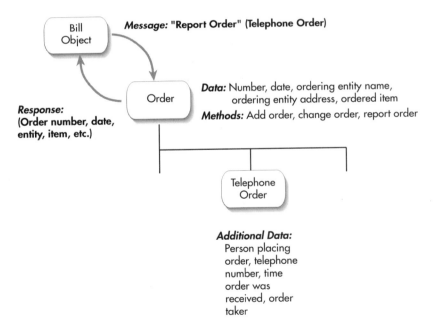

Figure 38: Object messaging

The order object class could itself be a *composite* object (as Figure 39 shows), constructed by linking an order number object, an ordering entity object, and an ordered item object (and perhaps others). This object is thus composed of multiple other objects in a key form of object reuse, and also presents one of the bigger problems in creating object-oriented systems—defining what is in one object versus another. In some ways, this is akin to defining entities in a data model. There are as yet no established methods for determining what constitutes a good object, rather than just being a part of an object or an object class. In fact, a major aspect of the art of object design rests in the ability of its practitioners to "factor" the application into objects appropriately.[3]

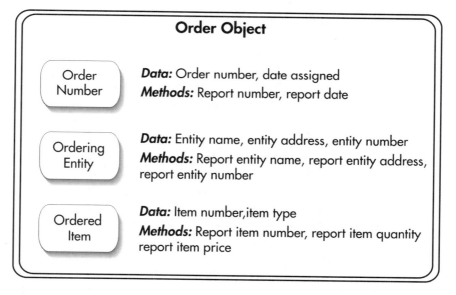

Figure 39: Object composition

---

3. The most experienced object practitioners have advanced the idea that all object development projects should have tasks for "refactoring" (i.e., reimplementing) the objects into other compositions or hierarchies since the first try is never good enough—good enough to yield a high performance system, good enough to yield objects that can easily be reused, good enough to yield all the maintenance benefits that we expect to get from the object approach. Refactoring is (currently) a fact of object life, but I have yet to see a development project that allows sufficient time in its plan for this activity.

Although modular interfaces are more explicitly defined with objects, object-oriented systems without inheritance and composition are not much more than what could be accomplished using more traditional tools and techniques. For this reason, object-oriented systems can be viewed as evolutionary to structured, modular systems. However, these additional properties of object-oriented systems significantly extend the concepts of modularity to include reuse of data and procedures to a very broad extent. Effective use of these properties (or others) should cause a sufficient change in the designer's basic thought processes and mind set to also view object orientation as somewhat revolutionary.

Portions of this section are based on an update of material in [Grochow 1991]

17.2 Objects and Data

When we talk of objects as "being composed of processing logic and data," we need to make the distinction between temporary and permanent data. Certainly, the working storage data is a part of every object, just as it is part of most non-object programs as well. However, this working storage may also represent the primary data of the application.

In our earlier examples of purchase order objects and employee objects, all of the data items listed (for example, the order number and the employee number) are physically stored as working storage variables within the order object (as Figure 40 illustrates). When the object is active in computer memory, each of those variables exists and has a value for a particular purchase order or employee. When we close the application, we have to store the objects somewhere to preserve the values of the data. In an object-oriented database, the entire object is stored on disk so the temporary data becomes permanent.

Most systems built today, however, do not use object databases, so the problem becomes more complicated. Most often, the object sends a message to a helper object to copy the temporary storage from the object in computer memory to more permanent storage in relational database tables, just as in a non-object system. In fact, there are several object class libraries that

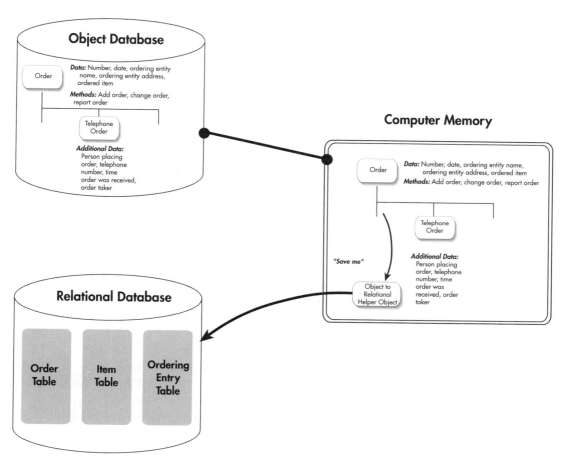

Figure 40: Object data storage

can now be purchased ("object middleware") to provide this function to the object programmer.[4]

---

4. It doesn't matter to the memory object whether the ultimate "permanent" database has an object structure or a relational structure, but it does matter to the object programmer that the message to store an object be a simple one.

17.3 THE SEEMING CONFLICT BETWEEN OBJECTS AND THREE-TIER CLIENT/SERVER

How can you have a three-tier client/server system and still use object technology?

Doesn't three-tier imply that the data is totally separated from the processing logic, and doesn't objects imply the opposite, that the data and the processing are combined into each object?

This confusion is often voiced, but its resolution is straight-forward: the "data" being referred to is different in each case.

In the case of three-tier client/server systems (as portrayed in Figure 11 on page 52), the "permanent" databases of the application are indeed separated from the general processing logic (and from the user interface logic). The order entry database, the personnel database, the customer master database, the open accounts database—all these are separated from the main application processing logic by defining interface programs that must be used to get access to them. In the case of object systems, these interface programs are the "helper objects" we talked about earlier.

All systems also have temporary data, reference data, and "working storage" data (the very temporary data used solely within a single application program) that are part of the application programs or objects. These are not separated from the application logic, nor are they considered a violation of the separation of processing logic and data implied in the definition of three-tier client/server systems.

 CONNECTIONS: *Three-Tier Client/Server and Objects*

So here we have the connection: each tier of a three-tier client/server system can use object technology. In the user interface tier, the objects represent particular items on the screen, such as windows, scroll bars, and pull-down lists. In the processing logic tier, the objects represent the things being processed, such as purchase orders, customer accounts, and payment vouchers (including their working storage). In the database tier, the objects are the helpers that surround the relational databases that are the permanent storage of the application.

Separation among the three tiers is maintained because only a few objects in one tier need to communicate with objects in another tier, and those communications are via "publicly" defined message formats ("publicly" at least within the realm of the application). As long as the message formats stay the same, the objects sending the messages will be independent of changes made in the processing logic or internal data structures of the objects receiving them.

18 Reusing Objects

Objects are seemingly a natural unit for reuse:[5] they are supposed to be well defined (via their external interface methods), easily accessible (via object class libraries), encapsulated (via hidden internals), and relatively portable. Unfortunately, too many of them (thousands) are required to create systems of any significant functionality, and they are often far too specialized in actual implementation to be reused in applications other than the ones they are designed for.

To better appreciate the issues in object reuse, we have to understand the two basic ways in which objects are reused. Gamma calls these "white-box reuse" and "black-box reuse" [Gamma 1995]. White-box reuse (based on the object property of "inheritance") is what most people actually think of when they talk about the new capabilities of the object approach, but it is black-box reuse (based on "object composition") that holds the most promise for simplifying system development.[6]

White-box reuse is reuse based on knowledge of the design and code of the objects to be reused. It is what designers and programmers do when they study generic object classes to determine how they might make them more specific

---

5. Actually, "object classes." It is the object class that defines the data and processes performed. The term "object"—when used in a formal sense—refers to a particular instance of an object class, i.e., one with specific data values being used in a specific operational environment of a specific system. "Person" is a typical object class in many systems; if I make an inquiry about "Jerry Grochow," then a specific instance of that class, the "Jerry Grochow object," will be created.

6. If you didn't understand this statement and you skipped Chapter 17 *A Brief Tutorial on Object Orientation* on page 115, ▼ now is a good time to go back and review.

for use in a particular system via the object inheritance mechanism. For example, an organization might have created a generic "person object class" with data such as name, social security number, and birthdate, as well as methods such as "report name," "report SSN," "report birthdate," and "report age" (along with a host of other housekeeping methods). A team creating a personnel system might want a person object that has all that, but also has employee number, hire date, and pension eligibility date, along with appropriate methods for accessing and updating. In white-box reuse, they would create a subclass of the person object (as shown in Figure 41) called "employee" that would contain only the additional data and methods. The rest would be inherited (i.e., executed) directly from the person object class.

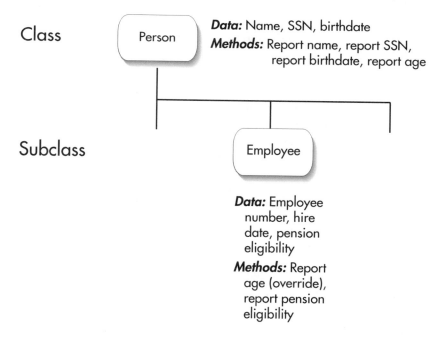

Figure 41: White-box reuse (object inheritance)

Creating this subclass requires a fairly detailed understanding of the way in which the "superclass" works. For example, if it is discovered that age is rounded or computed with some other simplifying assumption (everyone born in 1956 is reported as 40 years old in 1996, for example), this may not be sufficient for the personnel system, which needs age accurately to the half-year for analyzing pension eligibility. If that is the case, then the developers of the employee object class can override the "age method" of the person object class with one of their own. While the precision of the calculation should be specified in the documentation of the person object, more often it is necessary to look at the code of the method to find this out. In fact, the typical approach would be for the programmer to copy the code from the superclass and modify it as necessary, thus ensuring that any special conventions used in this system were carried forward in the new subclass. This admittedly simple example demonstrates that while objects are supposed to be "encapsulated" and known only through their externally defined methods, programmers need almost all the information about their internals in order to reuse them via the object inheritance mechanism (hence the label "white box reuse").

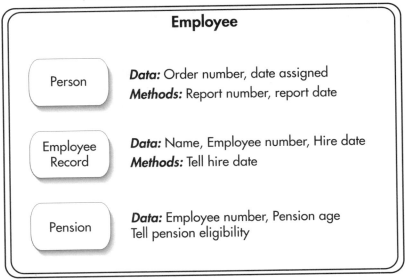

Employee

Person
Data: Order number, date assigned
Methods: Report number, report date

Employee Record
Data: Name, Employee number, Hire date
Methods: Tell hire date

Pension
Data: Employee number, Pension age
Tell pension eligibility

Figure 42: Black-box reuse (object composition)

In black-box reuse, the reuser creates new objects by assembly or composition. In this type of reuse in which objects are the building blocks used to construct more complex objects, the programmer is never modifying or replacing methods in the component objects and need only have knowledge of the messages that the objects expect to receive and process. Using this technique, for example, a programmer would create an employee object by combining (i.e., incorporating a reference to) the person object and other objects, such as an employment record object, a pension object, etc. Figure 42 shows this composite object. Because this approach does not rely on internal knowledge of each component object's code, it is less subject to breakage when changes are made within one of these component objects.[7]

Black-box and white-box reuse techniques can be combined to create new objects. In the example above, the pension object might be a subclass of a more generic employee benefit object from which it would have inherited various data and methods. The pension object would thus have been created using a white-box technique and then be used in the employee object via a black-box technique.

There is no formal rule for when to use black-box versus white-box techniques, and programmers will often develop personal preference for one or the other style. However, black-box techniques allow the creation of larger systems since complexity is hidden in lower layers of objects.[8]

The atomic unit of object programming is typically a small object, no more than a few dozen methods comprising a few

---

7. Some people have noted that this assembly approach is very similar to creating a traditional program as a "main program" calling a series of sub-programs which have been previously constructed. The similarity in structure is clear, except for the fact that the subprograms are often directly copied into the composite program, thus exposing their internal workings to scrutiny and possible direct modification. Of course, if this approach really worked with traditional programming languages, we might never have seen the intense interest in object languages. For some reason, this has mainly happened in the scientific and engineering domains and not in business and management domains.

8. See Chapter 20 *Why Are Object-Oriented Systems So Important?* on page 133 for further discussion on the topic of complexity.

hundred lines of code. If we are going to construct systems with the functionality equivalent to millions of lines of code, we have to find a way to deal with larger and larger units, that is, with composite objects. In some sense, the ideal composite object is actually an entire system that handles all aspects of a significant business function and that has been packaged for reuse by defining a limited number of external interfaces. This type of very large object is likely to be the atomic unit of "component assembly" programming in years to come.

 CONNECTIONS: *Objects, Components, Frameworks, and Reuse*

Objects grouped together into larger components or frameworks stand a better chance of being reused, particularly if the external interfaces to the entire framework are designed to make changes in most "internal" objects truly transparent to the reusing application. Objects specifically designed to be reusable, i.e., designed as general-purpose, have an even better chance.

18.1 AN ASIDE ABOUT THE HYPERBOLE OF OBJECT REUSE

While many claims have been made about the value of object reuse, and while most are intuitively appealing, there are also many that are clearly outrageous. An example from a marketing brochure of the consulting arm of a major computer manufacturer (name withheld to protect the guilty):

> *...As a result of our experience developing objects for your company, we will redesign and generalize those components for sale to others...Clients share in the royalty stream generated as objects are marketed for reuse. Clients should expect to recover all of their [CONSULTING GROUP] costs through harvesting and reselling via [NAME OF PARENT COMPANY] marketing channels...*

In today's software environment, this would appear to be a case of serious wishful thinking.

19
Three Views: In the Large, in the Medium, and in the Small

Some object programmers think of objects as only those very small units that define specific items such as a name, an address, or a list. Indeed, object language development environments come with object class libraries containing hundreds of such objects. A typical object in such a library may have only a few dozen methods of a dozen or so lines of code apiece, a total of a few hundred lines of code. But there are other views of what an object is, views that apply the basic principles that define objects to much larger units.

Take our ordering system again to exemplify all the possibilities: an order number can be an object (small), the entire order can be an object (medium), or the order entry system itself can be an object (large), as in Figure 43.

At AMS, we market an application called BureauLink® that handles all the communication and data manipulation necessary to contact any of the commercially available credit bureaus and perform basic analysis or retrieve a credit report, history, or analysis. We initially developed this system in conjunction with our own credit and collection system that we market to banks, telecommunications companies, and other organizations involved in billing and collecting. As we found more and more applications where BureauLink's function could be useful, we created a BureauLink "object." The BureauLink object represents the abstract class "credit report" and is totally modular and fully encapsulated (calling programs do not know how it is implemented). It understands a group of stan-

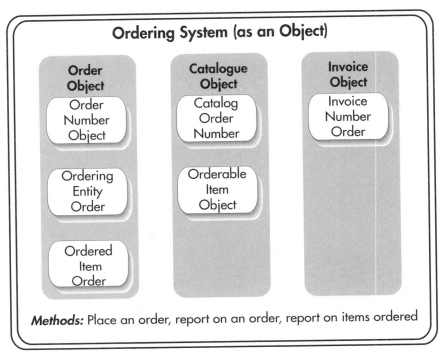

Ordering System (as an Object)

Order Object	Catalogue Object	Invoice Object
Order Number Object	Catalog Order Number	Invoice Number Order
Ordering Entity Order	Orderable Item Object	
Ordered Item Order		

Methods: Place an order, report on an order, report on items ordered

Figure 43: Different size objects

dard messages that you send in order to get it to perform its functions. For example, you send a message "retrieve standard credit report" to get it to contact a service bureau for the person being investigated, and you send it the same message regardless of the credit bureau you want to contact (a form of "polymorphism"). It is, for all practical purposes, an object—a very large object, but an object nonetheless.

CONNECTIONS: *Objects and Components*

Objects are often viewed as the base-level components of complex frameworks and applications. However, an entire application can itself be an object and a component of an even larger application. As we set our sights on applications measured in millions of lines of code, we will deal with components of increasing size if we are to keep their total numbers manageable. With appropriate attention to design, each of these components can indeed be viewed as a single composite object.

20 Why Are Object-Oriented Systems So Important?

So if objects are similar to programs, object programming similar to modular programming, and object technology "just" the next evolution of system development, why all the fuss? Theorists will ramble on about totally new ideas that will revolutionize the design and construction of systems; pragmatists will talk about the use of new programming languages and finally getting out from under the weight of COBOL. There are probably as many answers to why people are making a fuss as there are people answering the question. Here's mine.

Begin with these basic truths about systems:

- Systems get more complex with age (their age!) as end-users demand new functions and improved functionality.
- The more code you have to write, the more it costs (and the longer it takes) to develop and maintain the system.
- For the most part, systems professionals talk a different language than the end-users they are trying to help.
- It is impossible to determine complete specifications for a totally new system before that system is actually in production use.

Object technology is causing a fuss because it has a consequential impact on our response to all these points:

- *Dealing with complexity:*

Object technology is, pure and simple, an approach to managing complexity. And if we start with a less complex system, it will be easier to enhance and will stay less complex over time. With objects, a given functionality can be provided with less system-level complexity because the object becomes the unit of complexity, rather than the individual line of code. The idea of encapsulating code and data into objects creates a higher level programming unit, and creating more levels allows us to reduce complexity at any particular level. If we define a system's complexity to be related to the number of programming units that we have to deal with at a particular level, be they individual lines of code, objects, frameworks, or even larger components (each counting as one "complexity unit"), then we have now broken the relationship between more functionality and more complexity. If 100 lines of program code provides 1 unit of functionality but it takes only 1 object to provide that same unit of functionality, then we can use objects to add functionality with a much smaller increase in complexity than we could by writing more code. As Brad Cox recently wrote:

> *"...encapsulated complexity is no longer complexity at all. It's gone, buried forever in somebody else's problem." [Cox 1995]*

• *Reducing total lines of code written:*

The relationship between lines of code written and development and maintenance costs is clear to any IS manager. If we could find a way to develop applications without writing so much code (not just initially, but forever), we would have something worth making a fuss about. One obvious way to do this is to reuse code from one part of a system in another part of that same system or in another system entirely.[9] Subroutines, macro statements, and other techniques are a start in this direction, but

---

9. Of course, another obvious way is to "buy" the code rather than "build" it, and that is an increasingly utilized approach as we see more and more componentization of systems. The ultimate "buy" is to use a service bureau or to buy a complete package. Each approach has its own CONs to go with the PRO of having less code to maintain, so these are not necessarily universal solutions to the cost issue. I used to hear clients say that if a package didn't handle 80 percent of their requirements, it would be more pain than gain to use it. With the increasing complexity and costs of systems, organizations are taking another look at this and often incorporating packages that may initially handle only 50 percent of their perceived needs. It is still worth their while to use these packages as components of their overall system.

libraries of object frameworks is the more promising approach for improving reusability in larger systems.

- *Improving communications between developers and end-users:*

One of the tenets of object design is that real-world objects should become programming objects.[10] This means that discussions about vendors, purchase orders, telephone calls, and all the rest will begin in the early stages of system design and will continue right through programming. No longer will the discussion shift from talking about a payment voucher to talking about "module PV240"—the designer and programmer will be able to talk with the end-user about the payment voucher object and what it is supposed to do. Not only will some of the language barrier be broken down, but end-users will be drawn more completely into the development process. The eventual result can only be a system more directly meeting end-user needs and for which the end-users will feel more directly responsible.

Recently, the business processing engineering movement has taken up the call to objects. Implementing object-oriented analysis techniques allows the business process engineers to do their job in a way that is directly understandable to the software engineers. Taking an object approach to BPR deals with the very serious problem of ensuring that computer systems provide value by enabling and supporting the business process reengineering effort.

- *Dealing with incomplete and changing specifications:*

Iterative prototyping and incremental design go hand-in-hand with object development. These techniques, which grew out of the realization that specifications cannot be fully determined "up front," make it possible to meet the changing requirements of end-users.[11] End-users' understanding of which features are effective and useful will grow as they work with a system (or at least a prototype). With objects at the core of the system design,

---

10. As noted at the beginning of the section on objects, lots of objects will exist in the final system that do not represent "real-world" things, but here we are talking about the ones that do.

11. See *Iterative and Incremental Development* on page 197.

it is easier to modify and add to that design in an iterative way. With objects as the programming unit, it is easier to modify and add to the functioning system in an incremental way.

A study published in the *IBM Systems Journal* [Capper 1994] about three object projects carried out in 1991–92 is one of the few that attempted to measure and monitor the specific benefits of using object technology.[12] They report major positive impact on code quality, correctness, usability, adaptive maintainability (flexibility in meeting changing business requirements), and perfective maintainability.[13] Their "experiences in the three very different object-oriented projects confirm that this technology produces immediate benefits in many aspects of software quality and productivity." There is much anecdotal evidence of these benefits, and now there is starting to be at least some published quantitative data as well.

In the final analysis, any approach to developing systems is about increasing value. Modular approaches, structured design and programming, information engineering, and all the other techniques for reducing system complexity, simplifying development, and reducing maintenance are ultimately directed at increasing the value of our systems by reducing their cost and increasing their usefulness. We are starting to see some really large systems (in today's terms, typified by 10,000 function points or 1,000,000 lines of code or more) implemented using object-oriented techniques and incorporating libraries of reusable objects. In many cases, these systems could never have been attempted without object-oriented techniques to reduce complexity and allow incremental development. Some will undoubtedly fail to achieve their aims. But others will succeed. And that is what the fuss is all about.

20.1 Making Objects Universal Via Java

In 1993, I wrote an article entitled "Object's Bumpy Road" [Grochow 1993]. In it, I discussed the importance of object technol-

---

12. I have a few more things to say about the fact that so few of us are measuring things. See Chapter 38 *Measuring the New Information Systems Technology* on page 231.

13. They also saw some negative impact on performance, but that is another story.

ogy as well as the issues CIOs would face in attempting to use objects in large-scale, mission-critical business systems. Many of the same issues I talked about then are still with us now, such as how to develop large systems using thousands of objects, how to train existing designers and developers in the object approach, and how to plan for and manage large object development projects. However, object technology has become an accepted (although by no means universal) approach to systems development, with most major development methodologies incorporating object analysis and design, and most major programming languages and tools (including COBOL, Powerbuilder, and Visual Basic, as well as Smalltalk and C++) allowing us to generate reusable objects.

We are now seeing the stage being set for object technology to become universally accepted and for enough money to be spent to solve all its problems. The stage setting: the World Wide Web. The stage prop: Java.

I (and many others) believe that we are experiencing one of those rare events that is seminal in changing the direction of our industry. We know what those kinds of events are: the introduction of the IBM 360, the invention of the spreadsheet by Frankston and Bricklin, the development of the IBM Personal Computer, and most recently, the creation of the graphic World Wide Web browser by Marc Andreeson. In each case, the introduction of a single product set in motion a series of decisions in IS shops, in hardware and software vendors, and in the financial community that caused computerdom to take a significant turn: a turn toward standardization, a turn toward the desktop, a turn toward the network. In each case, it took us several years (more than five in the case of the IBM 360, one or two in the case of the Web browser) to recognize that turn had occurred. In each case, it took us—and is taking us—even longer to realize the full extent of the changes that had been set in motion.

The latest case, the introduction by Sun Microsystems of the Java programming language, seemed to be accompanied by almost instantaneous and widespread recognition of its implications for the development of new systems—potential implications, to be sure, but potential implications with the power to solve key problems of both the object world and, more generally, the client-server world. While I am most definitely not a language "bigot" (I don't really care what language you program in as long as you can create modular, reusable code that is really modular and really reusable), Java ignited a fire that no other language seemed to be able to. Undoubtedly, a large part of this conflagration is due to Java's being introduced as "the" language to turn the Web from a place for pretty pictures into the transaction-processing environment of the next century. But there are other reasons.

More has been written about Java in a shorter period of time than any other programming language in the history of digital computers (although a complete specification and language reference manual don't seem to have been among the writings). Some pundits have called it an "emasculated version of C + +," while others have noted that Java *is* C + +, but with the worst (and most troublesome) parts removed and the missing parts added. It is a language designed for "most" programmers to be able to produce small objects that can be combined quite readily into small applications that can be combined into bigger applications (no one really knows how big because the limits have not yet been explored). More important, those small applications, or "applets," can be downloaded to an end-user's machine (via the Internet or an Intranet) when they are needed, thus ensuring that thousands of desktops have consistent versions (the latest!) of your applications.

Perhaps most important, Java applications run in a virtual machine environment, via machine-independent "byte code" that is interpreted by a "virtual machine," an enabling program that can be running on any physical machine that someone has chosen to write it for. IBM, Apple, Hewlett-Packard, SCO, and Microsoft among others have all signed up to provide Java virtual machine environments on every piece of hardware and under every operating system that they can. These companies will help expand Java's use from its current niche as a language for Web programming, to its future role as a general purpose, universal programming language for all environments, venues, and applications. Indeed NorTel is using Java in its next generation telephones, and Sun is delivering an operating system that will run Java applications on almost any device that has a chip (read: everything electric!).

The not-so-hidden secret of this future is that the Java virtual machine environment could become the universal elixir of our industry. Since the specifications for the Java byte codes are readily available from Sun, anyone can write a version of any language compiler to produce Java byte code rather than native machine code. In short order, programmers will be able to use the language of their choice as their "development language" while that language's compiler produces truly machine-independent objects in Java byte code that can be run on every machine in the enterprise. Every language compiler for every language producing "byte code" that can be executed in any real machine's Java virtual machine environment—that's nirvana, and a universal object request broker as well.

Does Java have its faults? Most certainly, as would any nascent technological advance. In its interpreted (rather than compiled) incarnations, it is reported to run 10 to 20 times slower than C code. Programmers complain that available object classes are inadequate for many standard programming tasks—especially graphical user interface widgets. And full function development environments are just rolling off the programming line at most tool vendors. All of these problems will be solved in the next couple of years, but they clearly are problems right now.

While our industry has often been guilty of looking past today's problems to see tomorrow's advantages, those advantages are significant: machine independence, centralized management with distributed execution, a language that combines the benefits of a modular, structured, low-level language within the protected environment of a object-oriented virtual machine environment. While there are always nay-sayers, never before has a single approach to systems development had its support come from all three corners of the "globe," from Silicon Valley, from Armonk, and (somewhat grudgingly) from Redmond. Microsoft now promises Web browsers that will run Java better than Netscape, and IBM is making it available on the mainframe!

So maybe it isn't the object-orientedness of Java that is causing the press sensation, but the end result will still be that thousands of additional programmers will learn about objects and become imbued with the object approach. While I'm not quite so naïve as to believe that the transformation from the Tower of Babel to the Tower of Java will happen over night (what does in our industry?), or that such a transformation will be as smooth as Java's authors and supporters would have us believe, I do see that many forces are converging on our moving in its direction. Previous languages and development tools have incorporated one or more of Java's key concepts (objects, machine independent source code, hidden memory management, etc.), but none has garnered any significant industry support. For that, one has to credit Sun in recognizing that if Java were promoted as inexpensive and readily available, it would became accepted quickly—and Sun would make more money in the long run— than if they tried to take a more propriety approach.

So what is the probability of Java becoming the next COBOL (universally accepted and in use for more than 20 years)? Better than any other language or tool we have seen so far. Certainly, part of the world's current interest in Java is because of its association with programming for the World Wide Web, which is today everybody's favorite client/server platform. Java is, however, a true object-oriented language, it is easier to use than many others, and it is seeing an infusion of brain-power and money that almost guarantees long-term future interest. Java can indeed be the catalyst that turns object technology's bumpy road into a superhighway—and pave it all with applets.

Components Large and Small

Sometimes it helps to begin with Webster.[1] A *component* is "a constituent part" and *constituent* is here defined as "serving to form, compose, or make up a unit or whole." So a group of components make up the whole thing.[2]

---

1. And sometimes it doesn't, although most authors of descriptive texts will refer to this authority at least once, if not several times.

2. "Group of components" sounds somewhat inadequate and non-descriptive. Hundreds of terms exist in the English language to refer to groups of things, so perhaps we might find a better one. Alas, I have been unable to find an authority on which to base any particular usage, so here I invent my own: "court of components." *Court* is used to evoke the image of a group that is often cooperative and cohesive, but also allows for disagreement and dissent. While this is certainly more alliterative than *group* (or *number* or *bunch*), one might still question whether *court* is the appropriate term. As with other topics we are discussing, entire books have been written on this point, i.e., the naming of groups of things, or, as such words are more properly known, "terms of venery" (terms of hunting, since they were first used by huntsmen to distinguish different groups of animals). Most venery terms are collected in books hundreds of years old, although one modern book is available [Lipton 1991]. I suspect that most researchers in the components field will also be engaging in venereal pursuits in the hopes of making their own mark in the vocabulary. For me, I'll settle for *court*—at least for now.

But what thing? We can talk about the components of a client/ server system: its hardware components, its software components, its network components. If you are talking about the architecture of a client/server system, each workstation and each server is a component. If you are dealing with the application software, each major function may be a component. And if you are creating an object class library for resale, each class or group of related classes is a component.[3]

Use of the term "component" allows us to indicate that a thing is a part of a larger thing which is, therefore, composed of multiple sub-things, without indicating any other characteristic of the whole or the part. "Component" is a term that takes its specific meaning from the context in which it is used rather than being imbued with inherent meaning in and of itself. So, we can have large components and small components and components in between—in fact, we can have "components all the way down."[4] The term "component" is thus recursive: components can have components (of the same or different type) that have components, and so on.[5]

---

3. Indeed, Goldberg and Rubin [1995] take it to that level: "The objects that provide the general behaviors required by the application framework are called components of the framework" [p. 44]. One could go further by saying that the methods that constitute an object are its components, the lines of code that constitute the methods are its components, etc. It is not clear to me that this level of componentization has any practical significance to the IS practitioner.

4. I enjoy the story about a famous astronomer explaining the current view of the universe to a group of senior citizens. One adventurous person raised his hand to call the astronomer on his views and point out that really the Earth was resting on the back of a giant turtle. When the astronomer started to refute this by asking what the turtle was resting on, the questioner said, "I know where you're heading, sonny—it's turtles all the way down." Whether this really happened or not, the mythological turtles idea is a fascinating one.

5. We seem to like recursive definitions in information systems. An executive at IBM once told me that "to a chip designer, the 3090 mainframe is an application; to the 3090 designer, an operating system is an application; to an operating system developer, CICS is an application." I suspect that very few of the readers of this book would call any of these "an application," because their applications come at the next level down.

CONNECTIONS: Components, Components, Components

A key characteristic of the new information systems technology is the concept that systems should be viewed as being composed of and constructed from components. Whether we are talking about systems architecture, client/server, object technology, frameworks, or user interfaces—they can all be discussed in terms of their component parts. Once we understand this point, and the fact that components have components, we can talk about the value of the "component construction approach" and the issues that must be dealt with to use it to create valuable systems.

So why do I have so many footnotes on this section? Perhaps it is because so many diversions come to mind when talking about components. The less specifically something is defined, the more room one has for wandering. Or perhaps it is because a component approach to writing this section seemed most appropriate.

21 Components Have Components

Using a recursive definition of components (components are composed of components…), we can look at a system from many levels to see what its components are at that level. For example, at the top or "system level," a system is composed of hardware components (computers), network components (local and wide-area networks), and software components (user interface, major business functions, and database processing). Moving down a couple of levels, the software "user interface component" might include menu, help, and work-flow components. And so on down the line.

Figure 44 shows the major hierarchical levels that can be created when analyzing the components and sub-components of a system. Figure 45 takes each level, beginning with the system itself, and shows some of the types of sub-components that might be seen at the next level down, as well as indicating what a view of that particular level might be used for. As you can see, there are many ways to view the componentization of a system (i.e., the levels of its components). Be assured that someone on your project team will find a reason to take each view of components and maybe even some others!

The sections that follow focus primarily on software components, whose appropriate use is perhaps the greatest challenge in creating value with the new information systems technology.

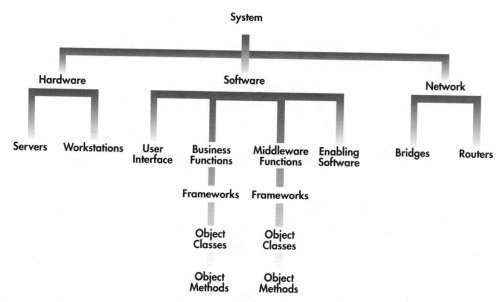

Figure 44: Components have components

Figure 45: Sub-component views

Component Level	Sub-Component Types	Uses of this Level View
System	Hardware, major software functions, network	System overview
Software	Application subsystems	Functional overview
Software (another view)	Layers, tiers	Software architecture review
Software layers, tiers	Application functions, middleware functions, enabling software, etc.	Detailed software architecture review
Application or middleware function	Frameworks	Detailed functional analysis
Application framework	Object classes	Detailed framework analysis
Object class	Methods	Detailed object analysis

Figure 45: Sub-component views (Contd)

Component Level	Sub-Component Types	Uses of this Level View
Hardware	Computers, printers, disks, tapes, etc.	Detailed hardware analysis
Network	Routers, bridges, multiplexors, etc.	Detailed network analysis

21.1 AN HISTORICAL VIEW OF SOFTWARE COMPONENTS

Although computer hardware has always been constructed from components, software was, until relatively recently, built as if it were a monolithic whole. Not many years ago, the only two software components were the operating system and the application. In fact, we loaded the operating system (and occasionally our customized changes to it) right along with the application—in the same deck of cards—as a single program "component." As time went on, developers came to trust that they could use the standard operating system loaded once at the beginning of the day, and they stopped loading it as an integral part of each application run. The operating system became the first stand-alone software component.

If you were writing a scientific program, you may have added a scientific subroutine library to your deck to provide the program code that performed various complex calculations. After a while, it too was loaded once and shared by all users. Today's software component architectures are the descendants of this burgeoning approach to segmenting software into more and more modules that could be used by more than one program or more than one person.

From the point at which it was accepted that the operating system could be viewed as a standard component available to all, the industry rapidly progressed to accept database management systems, teleprocessing monitors, and other "system-level" components. This was the state of affairs until the early 1970s, when organizations began to realize that at least some of their most common application functions, e.g., payroll and accounting, could be treated as components and that they should consider purchasing these off-the-shelf from outside vendors. Given the hundreds of vendors in today's application software marketplace, end-user organizations found this approach highly desirable, regardless of the headaches that it was causing in their IS departments.

The IS department had to deal with application components because it couldn't keep up with the demand for new functionality that end-users wanted. Even though these packages didn't quite do exactly what they wanted and didn't quite fit into their existing technical environments, IS management had to consider this less-than-optimal (from the IS point of view) approach. As software package vendors sold more and more copies of their products, they added more and more features and supported more and more technical environments. Over time, the benefits of buying applications as the top-level components of complex application environments became the norm. It was only in the largest organizations and for the most complex business functions that new applications were developed from scratch.[6]

As systems architectures have become more complex, the need for additional types of components has grown. In particular, the concept of "middleware," software that sits between the operating system layer and the application function layer, has become very popular in the 1990s. Middleware is a direct result of the complexity of the operating environments in that it tries to hide much of that complexity from the application programmer (see the following section).

The logical extension of the componentization of the operating systems layers is the componentization of the application layer. Rather than viewing the application as a single component, some organizations are today viewing it as potentially being composed of components as well. What they are looking for is the creation of larger and smaller components of application function that can be readily updated or exchanged—or purchased.

---

6. It should be noted that this "build from scratch" market is still booming—but so is the application package market. It is in the merger of these two approaches, i.e., using packages as components of even larger custom-built systems, that the future lies (and where my employer gets the majority of its revenues already).

Brad Cox, one of the early pioneers of the object approach to development, believes that the future of the software industry lies with a large number of component manufacturers supplying "software ICs" (he uses the integrated circuit industry as an analogy) to those of us who assemble them into applications [Cox 1992]. Although the eventual outcome is still unclear, there are many indications that our industry is moving in this direction.[7] It is how we will be providing multi-million line-of-code systems that allow end-users to access highly sophisticated functions through easy-to-use interfaces—without having to deal at the level of each of those lines of code.

---

7. This trend is important not only for what it brings to software development directly (improved flexibility and productivity) but also for what it implies about the structure of organizations. First, it implies that there will be more and more suppliers of software and that IS shops will have to take on some of the characteristics of manufacturing organizations in dealing with large numbers of suppliers or distributors. And it implies that learning how to deal with suppliers will be one of the critical success factors in implementing systems in the future. See Chapter 24 *The Component Approach Creates an IS Technology Supply Chain* on page 160.

22 Component Layers and Tiers ▼

It is not uncommon in today's software environment to have literally hundreds of components, often organized into layers and tiers. Layers and tiers consist of components (programs or objects) that work together to perform a larger function.[8] Defining the software architecture as composed of related layers and tiers is the first step in identifying the component structure of the system.

A software layer is typically designed to contain related modules that mostly interact with each other rather than with modules in another layer. Each layer then has a small number of interfaces (object methods, subroutine calls, language verbs, or the like) that are referenced by components from another layer. Software tiers are similarly composed of modules that work together. Typically several tiers work in parallel as a layer. (You have already seen these concepts introduced in Chapter 13 *Defining System Architecture* on page 83)

Layers are most often shown in diagrams as horizontal rectangles to indicate that components in "higher" or "lower"-level layers interact only with components in the adjacent layers. Tiers are portrayed vertically to indicate related functions interacting with other tiers within the same layer. Figure 30 (repeated below as Figure 46) is a an example schematic of a tiered and layered component software architecture (with tier detail shown for two of the layers).

In this figure, the database management system (DBMS) provides services "up" to the components of the application common services layer while calling "down" upon services of the components of the operating system layer.

---

8. Frameworks are also composed of components that work together to perform a larger function. They are most often associated with object technology and are discussed in Chapter 23 *Patterns, Templates, and Frameworks* on page 153

Programs in the application function tiers should not have to call upon services in the operating system directly—they should all be provided through the application common services via the database manager.

This type of layered and tiered application architecture approach has proven useful in hundreds of applications across all functional areas in hundreds of organizations. Experience shows that strict isolation of each level is a somewhat idealized concept (as was discussed under Section 15.1 *System "Logical" Architecture* on page 96), but this is a normal translation of a useful theoretical construct into actual practice.

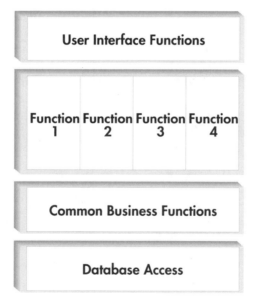

Figure 46: Components in layers and tiers

22.1 MIDDLEWARE

Middleware is yet another term with a somewhat fuzzy definition. Literally, it is applied to software "in the middle," software that isolates application functions from operating system and network functions. Various authors have included teleprocessing monitors, database management systems, network protocol stacks, remote procedure calls, and other network-related functions in the middleware layer. *Computerworld's Client/Server Journal* periodically publishes a "client/server infrastructure road map" listing various types of middleware. Figure 48 is my interpretation of their categories (based on [CWCSJ 1995]).[9]

Figure 47: Example of middleware categories

Category	Purpose	Example
Remote procedure call	Call to procedure running on another computer	OSF DCE, Sun ONC RPC
Interprocess communication	Handles sending messages from one program to another across separate process spaces	Named pipes, Windows sockets
Message-oriented middleware	Isolates the process sending a message from the process receiving it; a form of interprocess communication	IBM MQSeries, PeerLogic PIPES
Message routing	Handles addressing and routing across wide area networks	Microsoft MAPI, X.400
Distributed directory services	Handles naming and addressing of system components in a distributed environment	OSF DCE Global Naming
Distributed security services	Handles security and access control in a distributed environment	OSF DCE Kerberos
Distributed time services	Handles time synchronization in a multi-computer environment	OSF DCE Time Service

9. See also [Hessinger 1994] in the excellent but not widely available journal *MiddlewareSpectra* (formerly *OTM [Open Transaction Management] Spectrum,* formerly *Open Systems Spectrum* née *SAA Spectrum*—this magazine keeps up with the times!).

Figure 47: Example of middleware categories (Contd)

Category	Purpose	Example
Teleprocessing monitors	Handles synchronization of transactions and data in a system where events occur asynchronously	IBM CICS, Transarc Encina, Novell Tuxedo
Object request broker	Makes it possible for one object to send a message to another object without knowing the name of the ultimate target object or where it resides	IBM SOM/DSOM, SunSoft DOE, various implementations of OMB CORBA standard

You will note that many different categories of middleware seem to provide similar services, specifically sending information back and forth between programs. If you are already familiar with some of the products that occupy this niche, you will recognize the important role that they serve. Suffice it to say that this is an extremely complex set of tasks to deal with in an arbitrarily distributed computer system. It is not unusual for any one of these components to itself be composed of dozens of sub-components; in total, to comprise a million lines of code, and to require programmers to learn hundreds of interface definitions to use all its features (for example, the Distributed Computing Environment defined by the Open Software Foundation).[10] In fact, some middleware is so complex that practitioners are now talking about "upper middleware" and "lower middleware," with the former to hide some of the complexity of the latter. This appears to be a normal progression of providing successive layers of software to hide increasing layers of detail.

Once again, we cannot simply rely on our understanding of a label like "middleware" to know how a system is constructed, or even what it is composed of. Detailed architecture diagrams showing the contents of the middleware layer are almost always necessary if you really want to see what software components are present and how they are being used.

---

10. To find out more about OSF, check out their site on the World Wide Web at http://www.osf.org.

23 Patterns, Templates, and Frameworks

The computer field has always taken terms from the general lexicon to describe what it is all about—but then put a twist on common meanings so that only practitioners really understand the usage. That seems to be the case with three terms that have been used sporadically over the years but have re-entered our vocabulary with a vengeance: *patterns, templates,* and *frameworks*. Some confusion still remains even among practitioners as to what they mean in the context of the new information systems technology, and what distinguishes one from the other in the context of new information systems development. Simply put:

- *Patterns* are written descriptions of solutions to common programming problems, documented in a standardized way.

- *Templates* are generic program code (performing common functions) that can serve as the basis for developing specific program code for your applications.

- *Frameworks* are programs (more and more delivered as sets of cooperating object classes) performing some set of general functions that can be directly integrated into your application system (examples are given below). [11]

The concept underlying each term is that systems can be developed more effectively and efficiently if a body of design specifications and code is available that can be used over and over, just as common designs and parts are available to engineers in other disciplines. When we all learn common design and programming patterns in school,

---

11. If you haven't figured out what objects are all about yet, skip ahead to the next section, or if you have more time, read David Taylor's excellent introduction to the subject [Taylor 1990].

when we all incorporate common frameworks in our systems, when we all reuse common templates in our code, then we will be able to say that software development has become an engineering discipline. The software engineer's job is to find, invent, and develop the patterns, templates, and frameworks that provide the most value in constructing specific systems.

CONNECTIONS: *Objects, Patterns, Frameworks, and Templates*

We are seeing heightened interest in patterns, frameworks, and templates with the popularization of object technology. Objects give us the components for delivering frameworks and templates and for specifying patterns. Although a single object is too small a unit to consider as the "atomic element of reuse" (tens of thousands of them would be needed), a framework or template consisting of a number of objects can be much more understandable and manageable. For most purposes, it is not necessary to understand the details of the objects within the framework and it is the framework, that becomes the atomic element of reuse.

23.1 PATTERNS

Gamma and his co-authors (affectionately known as the "Gang of Four" among inhabitants of the patterns discussion on the Internet) provide THE sourcebook for defining the concept of a pattern as well as for providing a major contribution to the documentation of key technical patterns used in creating object-oriented systems [Gamma 1995]. "Design patterns" are the abstract definition and documentation of "communicating objects and classes that are customized to solve a general design problem in a particular context" [p. 3]. In other words, patterns are general designs of solutions to common system design problems.

The key contribution pattern enthusiasts are making is the enforced documentation in a common format of recurring design solutions that will contribute to a body of software engineering knowledge. This is not a new idea. Donald Knuth undertook a massive effort to document approaches to such problems as sorting and parsing in the 1970s [Knuth 1973].[12] The *Design Patterns* book itself documents over twnety patterns in a catalog that runs almost 300 pages, and other authors have created dozens more. In effect, people who document patterns are creating the raw material that will eventually make software design and development into an engineering discipline.[13]

23.2 TEMPLATES

Another term sometimes associated with new component construction techniques is "templates." In the systems development arena, the word *template* carries a slightly different meaning than it does in common usage (where it typically means a pattern). In current systems parlance, a template is a skeleton of some function that needs to be fleshed out by the designer or programmer. The distinction is that the pattern is a complete (written) solution to a particular problem, whereas the template is only a skeleton (in programming code).

In the case of a system with many similar programs, the lead programmer commonly develops a program template and gives it to the other programmers. The template might include the data definitions, the basic control flow (paragraphs and blocks), initialization code, and termination code. All the programmers have to do is to fill in the specific code for predetermined opera-

---

12. Knuth planned six volumes of which only three have been completed so far, but they were (and are) a major contribution to the study of computer programming. Knuth also has a wonderful sense of humor, having included (without attribution) a statement of Fermat's Last Theorem as one of the exercises at the end of the first chapter. In the answer section at the back of the book, he said that a friend of his had an elegant proof but it was too big to fit in the space available. What other answer could have been more appropriate?

13. Coupled with the Internet as a publishing medium, this effort by literally hundreds of researchers and practitioners to document design patterns will become the "sourcebook" of software engineering. Check out the Portland Patterns Repository at http://c2.com/ppr/index.html, the Patterns Page at http://st www.cs.uiuc.edu/users/patterns/patterns.html, and the Patterns Handbook (to download) at ftp://ftp.oi.com/pub/oi/books/stpthlp.zip.

tions at predetermined points in the template program.[14] A similar approach can be taken with design templates, for example in designing a set of windows with common characteristics.

Templates thus fill another role in the firmament of reusable software componentry. They provide coding examples that developers can use in implementing standardized solutions to their programming tasks.

23.3   FRAMEWORKS

The concept of frameworks is not particularly difficult, although we sometimes try to make it appear so. Here are what some of the industry's leading gurus and organizations have to say about frameworks.

> *A framework is a set of prefabricated software building blocks that programmers can use, extend, or customize for specific computing solutions... Frameworks are built from a collection of objects, so both the design and code of a framework may be reused. [Taligent 1994]*

> *An application framework is a set of objects that interact to form the basic structure and processing of applications within a given domain. [The framework is defined] in sufficiently general or abstract terms, so that we can change the object that provides the expected behavior without changing the implementation of the basic application itself. This extends the usefulness of the application. [Goldberg and Rubin 1995]*

> *A framework is a set of cooperating classes that make up a reusable design for a specific class of software...You customize a framework to a particular application by creating application-*

---

14. At AMS, we have been using this technique for as long as I can remember. Over the years, we developed hundreds of document, processing systems (order entry, accounting, payroll, etc.), all following the same basic pattern (common definition): process the document header, process each line on the document, process the document footer. We created a generic document framework that included program templates for key data entry and editing programs. This approach allowed us to train relatively inexperienced programmers to be productive in a very short period of time and to amaze our clients and competitors with our software wizardry. Most successful software development organizations now follow this approach in at least some of their programming efforts.

*specific subclasses of abstract classes from the framework.
[Gamma 1995, p.26]*

*Frameworks refer to collections of concrete classes working
together to accomplish a given parameterizable task. [Viljamaa
1995]*

So, a framework is (simply) a generalized backbone for a certain
application function, implemented as objects. Using frameworks simplifies applications in two ways: first, they provide
code that doesn't have to be written from scratch; second, they
provide a common structure and form for applications that
makes these applications simpler to understand—and maintain
over time.

The researchers at Taligent Corporation (now incorporated
into the IBM Corporation) divided frameworks into three types:

- *Application frameworks,* which support the functions
  needed by a wide variety of applications, such as a GUI
  framework.
- *Domain frameworks,* which "encapsulate expertise in a
  particular problem domain" by providing a common set of
  functionality, such as credit checking used in banking and
  other commercial systems.
- *Support frameworks,* which "provide system-level services,
  such as file access, distributed computing support, or
  device drivers."

To round out this definitional discussion, we should note that
Gamma and his fellow authors use the term "toolkit" to distinguish a different class of reusable code. They make the distinction that a toolkit is somewhat like a sub-routine library in that
you write the main body of code yourself and then call (or
incorporate) the code from the toolkit. A framework, on the
other hand, "dictates the architecture of your application,"
defining the overall structure and the thread of control. You start
with the framework, then fill in parameters and additional code
to make it work for your application. In their definition, toolkits
and frameworks are somewhat at opposite ends of a spectrum:
with a toolkit, you focus on reusing the code; with a framework

you concentrate on reusing the design. However, these subtle distinctions about naming often get lost in common practice.

The CommonPoint Application System from Taligent Corporation [Taligent 1995] is an example of a set of frameworks designed to work together in providing a flexible environment for creating many types of applications. The CommonPoint frameworks include such titles as desktop workspace, compound document, shared document, presentation, graphics editing, text editing, user interface, international text, time-based media (e.g., audio and video), file interoperability, and software portability. Figure 48 shows several of the CommonPoint frameworks classified according to type of framework.

Figure 48: Example Taligent CommonPoint frameworks

Framework Type	Framework Name	Example Functions
Application	Desktop Workspace	Drag and drop, document proxy
	Compound Document	Embedding and linking, in-place editing, multi-level undo/redo
Domain	Graphics	Integrated 2-D and 3-D geometries, rendering, shading
	International Text	Date/currency/time/numeric formats, language-sensitive word breaks
Support	File Interoperability	Format translation, clipboard
	Distributed Computing	Concurrency control, recovery, licensing, directory services

Figure 49 shows another example, this one from the realm of a business application. It shows some of the frameworks used in the development of a suite of applications for a securities trading firm.

Figure 49: Types of frameworks comprising a business application

Type of Framework	Examples
Domain	Interest calculation, trade detail verification, stock records posting, collateral management, tax posting
Application	Security, encryption, error processing, multi-currency processing
Support	Workflow, queue management, batch processing, entity locking, object persistence, database translation

This example shows frameworks that would be incorporated in both the application and middleware layers of the system's architecture. The "support frameworks" in the example would be shown in the middleware level of the systems architecture, performing services that rely heavily on operating system functions that are then hidden from the application business function. Middleware frameworks are typically purchased as reusable components from third-party software vendors, rather than being developed by project teams working on application systems.

Regardless of whether you distinguish toolkits from frameworks from templates from subroutine libraries, the important point is that well-understood, reusable, generalizable components are necessary for us to implement the increasingly sophisticated systems that our organizations are demanding.

24

The Component Approach Creates an IS Technology Supply Chain

> *The linkages between suppliers' value chains and a firm's value chain provide opportunities for the firm to enhance its competitive advantage...Supplier linkages mean that the relationship with suppliers is not a zero sum game in which one gains only at the expense of the other, but a relationship in which both can gain.*
>
> Michael Porter, *Competitive Advantage,* p. 51

In many ways, the rise of the new information systems technology parallels the significant changes that have been occurring in the structure of the IS industry over the past decade. What was an industry dominated by a few global suppliers of both hardware and software (IBM and DEC come to mind) has become a veritable bazaar with hundreds of vendors, many of whom produce only a single type of hardware, software, or network product. What was an industry characterized by proprietary systems is now one characterized by systems with supposedly interchangeable parts supplied by multiple vendors. What was an industry in which we could count on systems performing in an understandable and repeatable way has become one in which we must constantly test, tune, fiddle, and reintegrate components that may not do the same thing twice in a row.

The implications of these changes are enormous and directly impact information system professionals and end-users everywhere. Where it used to be possible to buy a complete computer system (both hardware and software) from a single vertically integrated vendor, that is effectively impossible today, and the more likely case is that a dozen suppliers in a horizontal supply chain will be involved. IS organizations are just beginning to understand the types of changes they must make in their own structure and management to operate effectively in this world of expanding "technology supply chains"—something that manufacturing organizations, particularly in the auto industry, have recently seen as a major factor in competitive survival.

As to client/server systems, the technology supply chain is the network of organizations providing the components and subcomponents that make up the system. If you were able to purchase a complete working system from a single vertically integrated vendor, call it Galactic Systems Corporation (or Galacticorp for short), then the supply chain would appear to be simple: from Galacticorp to you. But even a behemoth such as Galacticorp would have suppliers, companies that provide it the

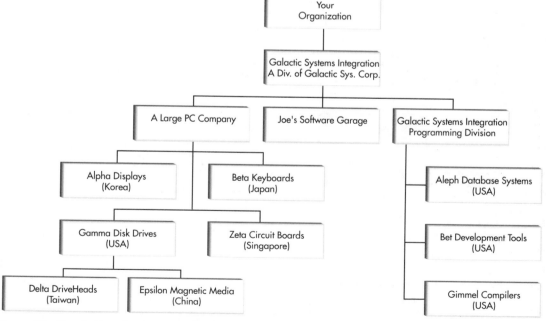

Figure 50: Simple IS technology supply chain

raw materials (or not-so-raw materials, such as integrated circuit chips) for producing its systems (as Figure 50 shows). If you look closely, the technology supply chain gets longer and longer.

If Galacticorp has a systems integration arm (which it most surely would), it can insulate you from the next layers in the supply chain. As far as you are concerned as a client of Galacticorp, *it* is the only supplier you ever have to deal with. It makes most of the real supply chain invisible (as depicted in Figure 51)—exactly as it was when you were dealing with IBM or DEC in the 1980s (and as is done for most manufactured goods that we buy today).

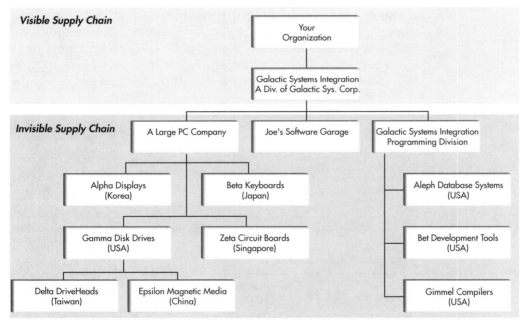

Figure 51: Visible and invisible parts of the supply chain

In the 1980s, it was highly likely that a typical IS shop in a Fortune 1000 company was running an IBM (or DEC) application on an IBM operating system on an IBM computer over an IBM network to an IBM terminal. Even though IBM had contracted out for some of its components or subsystems (even some of its operating systems), this was effectively hidden from their customers because IBM took responsibility for delivering a complete solution and solving any problems that may have arisen. It was the only supplier that was visible to you.

IS shops had it relatively easy back then: they dealt with one primary vendor (or at most two) and relied on it unquestioningly to solve all problems. But we didn't like that—it made us too dependent on the whims of a single organization. So we changed it and created today's world of "open" client/server systems. This is a world where we serve in the role of systems integrator or at least participate in making supply chain decisions (even if we have another organization assume the systems integrator role for us). We are constantly choosing whose hardware we will use, whose database, whose network. We decide, among the various suppliers of each component, whether we want Oracle, Sybase, Informix, or another. We may even decide on the keyboards we want on our PCs. We establish the way we want to deal with suppliers, in an arm's-length relationship, in a partnership, or something in between. We take on the task of creating and dealing with a highly visible direct supply chain (as Figure 52 shows).

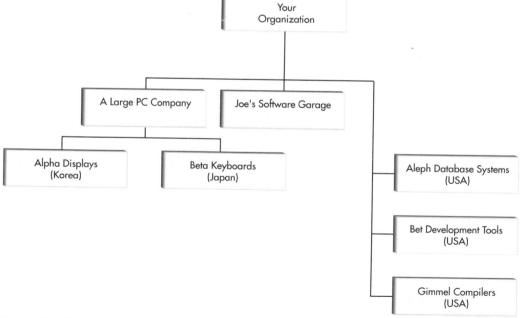

Figure 52: Direct supply chain

Remember, we wanted this. It removes our dependence on the single vertically integrated supplier. It gives us freedom of choice. It gives us competitive leverage.[15] Yet, the most frequently cited obstacle to successful implementation in the client/server environment in the previously cited Deloitte & Touche survey is "the complexity of the multi-vendor environment" [Plewa and Pliskin 1995]. What this means is that we haven't yet figured out how to take advantage of the component approach and the supply chain that it creates—we are still fighting it.

Taking advantage of the supply chain means that we have to acknowledge it and start taking explicit action to harness it. If we want to create value from the new information systems technology, we must understand how to create effective IS technology supply chains—there is no alternative except return to dealing with a single vertically integrated manufacturer (more on this alternative later).

24.1 THE EXPANDING SUPPLY CHAIN PROBLEM

DILBERT ©1996. United Features Syndicate.   Reprinted by Permission.

We can learn to take advantage of the technology supply chain. It is already being done, in our industry and others. Prof. Joseph Badaracco of the Harvard Business School has done extensive

---

15. It also gives us migraine headaches. There is a reason why profit margins are relatively low in most systems integration companies.

research in this area for his book *The Knowledge Link* [Badaracco 1991].

> *Abundant evidence shows how frequently alliances are blurring firms' boundaries. During the 1980s, the number of domestic U.S. joint ventures increased rapidly. The greatest changes occurred in service industries such as advertising, financial services, communications systems and services, and data base development and management. Cooperation also burgeoned among manufacturers of electrical equipment, consumer electronics, computer peripherals, software, electrical components, and aerospace products. In some of these sectors, more domestic joint ventures were announced in a single year of the early 1980s than in the previous 15 or 20 years. [p. 5]*

To begin, we have to understand more about the problems we will face. Three factors contribute to the scope of the technology supply chain problem:

1. With the introduction of client/server computing, the total number of vendors' products involved in a single "system" has increased dramatically.

2. The number of vendors that the internal IS organization has to deal with directly (the visible supply chain) has increased.

3. The average size of those vendors has decreased.

As discussed above, today's IS shop has direct contact with at least a dozen manufacturers and often many more. Microsoft notwithstanding, we are in an industry characterized by multiple suppliers for each component of the "system." Furthermore, systems are being modularized and decomposed into more and more components, thus allowing more and more suppliers to enter a niche in the marketplace.

Take a typical business application developed by a systems integrator or consultant using custom software as well as third-party components. The developers may have used several computer languages coming from such major suppliers as IBM or Microsoft, or smaller companies such as ParcPlace or Digitalk (Smalltalk), or medium-sized companies such as Symantec or Borland (C + +). They may have used tools and incorporated run-time libraries from vendors such as Gupta, Powersoft, Microfocus, Rational, and a dozen others you probably never heard of. The application is probably running on an operating system from Microsoft (although it may be on one from IBM, Sun, SCO, or several others) on a computer from Compaq or Dell connected to a network from Novell accessing a database from Sybase or Oracle running on a machine from Hewlett-Packard or Sun. In the *Client/Server Journal* client/server infrastructure road map [CWCSJ 1995], some 30–40 significant components are shown (depending on how you count), each with from four to several dozen suppliers of competing products.

Numbers notwithstanding, it is the size of the vendors that is sometimes most troubling to the large organizations trying to develop component-based systems. The suppliers of those components are invariably smaller organizations than those they sell to, some as small as two developers and an assistant. Picture walking into the CEO's office to present your strategy for development of "the" system that is going to make or break the company's business. Not that you will spend much time on the fact that it is the company's first implementation of a client/server, object-oriented, component-based approach, but you will, of course, mention all the vendors that you will be depending on to make this happen. There is IBM, Microsoft, Oracle (or Sybase)— all companies that are well known to today's computer-aware executive. But then there is also Advanced MicroCompuWare, Avocado Systems, and Beetlebung Software.[16] You will be betting your company's future on the fact that these organizations will be around to update their products to meet your needs for a long time into the future.

Whether it is the internal IS shop or an external consultant or system integrator who brings all these components together, today's environment makes it practically impossible for the integrator to take complete responsibility for the effective working of the system. When an error is traced back to the language

---

16. Any naming resemblance to real companies is purely accidental. It is, however, difficult to come up with inventive names as the number of companies feeding our software and hardware habits seems to increase without bound.

compiler or the operating system (or sometimes even the hardware), about all they can do is search frantically for a workaround. The IS department (and even the end-user) is painfully aware of these issues and, unfortunately, must deal with them—something they never had to do before.

24.2 Why Is the Supply Chain Expanding?

The IS technology supply chain continues to expand. It is increasing in both breadth (the number of vendors supplying components) and depth (the number of "nested" suppliers), and organizations have to deal with both of these factors.

There are many reasons for the increasing supply chain, but key factors are these.

- Systems are more complex, and no one firm can have all the knowledge necessary to develop it all. Buying components is one way of gaining access to specialized knowledge.[17]
- The industry is fraught with labor shortages, and buying components (using capital, rather than labor) is one way of dealing with a labor shortage.
- While organizations can learn to use new technologies, tight time frames for implementing new systems often dictate buying components or expertise to reduce time to market.
- When multiple approaches are available to developing or architecting new systems, organizations can reduce risk and save time by buying proven solutions.
- Tooling up to work with new technologies takes a significant capital investment. Buying solutions based on those technologies from the outside can reduce that capital investment.
- With increased competitive pressures, organizations are focusing their attention on those areas that are felt to be

---

17. As Bill Joy, outspoken founder of Sun Microsystems, is reported to have said: "Let's be truthful; most of the bright people don't work for you—no matter who you are. You need a strategy that allows for innovation occurring elsewhere." [*Forbes Magazine "ASAP,"* August 28, 1995, p. 146]

key to their business success. If information systems development is not considered to be a "core competence," they will look outside for assistance.

Supply chains are being created for all these reasons and others.[18]

24.3 LESSONS TO BE LEARNED

We can learn a lot from the manufacturing firms that have been focusing on unlocking the value in their technology supply chains and their successes and failures. Some of the lessons they have learned about reducing costs, improving quality, and reducing cycle times are now being implemented by forward-thinking organizations and by the systems integrators they work with.

Much of the current thinking about supply chains has emerged from studying the Japanese auto industry and their style of *lean production*. "Lean production" is a term coined by the International Motor Vehicle Program team at MIT [Womack 1990] to encompass all the processes that the Japanese auto industry put in place to become competitive in world markets. Lean production is what allows Japanese automobile assemblers, and more recently the semiconductor manufacturers and even some automobile assemblers in the United States, to produce products that consumers want, at a price they are willing to pay, at a quality that keeps them satisfied, while making a profit that is acceptable to the company's shareholders.

One key strategy of lean production is extremely close working relationships between vendors and manufacturers, i.e., between component suppliers and component assemblers. In the Japanese auto industry, it is not uncommon for engineers from the major assemblers (Honda, Nissan, Toyota) to be on assignment in the R&D organizations of their suppliers. Rather than being hampered in their relationship by concerns about

---

18. Badaracco goes beyond these reasons to discuss strategic motives. His thesis is that the "globalization of knowledge" is causing companies to form alliances of many forms. Clearly this is true, but it is questionable whether more than a few organizations currently take this broad a view of their corporate relationships.

competitive secrets, they are working together in an atmosphere of trust and openness.

This side-by-side working relationship is the opposite of the somewhat-secretive vendor-supplier relationship that until recently typified the American automobile industry. It is a strategy that ensures the compatibility of the hundreds of parts that are assembled into a working automobile and in large measure has eliminated the need for huge end-of-assembly-line rework departments ("debugging") to deal with parts incompatibilities—something that is anathema to high-efficiency, high-quality production processes.

The same lean and "trustful" approach implemented in the Japanese automobile industry (and more recently emulated in Detroit) must be implemented among IS organizations and their software and hardware suppliers. This is the only way we will significantly reduce the high cost of system integration and the need for on-going "proof of technical architecture" departments. Although the level of consumer-supplier cooperation today is often seen as necessitating little more than sending several programmers to an annual user's conference, many developers are supplementing this once-a-year contact with on-going communication in cyberspace, via the Internet or via vendor-supported forums on Compuserve and American Online. This results in an almost immediate feedback and support cycle, one of significantly higher value to both parties because of its immediacy.

At the next level, some software suppliers have customer councils and feedback sessions, but they are generally infrequent and typically present high-level product plans, divulging as little information as possible to satisfy their customers that they are being open to input, and without any stated commitment to act on the results of the discussions. More-enlightened software vendors go one extra step of agreeing to incorporate certain of the suggestions made from these customer councils into future releases of their products, but even then without committing to delivery date or details. These arm's-length customer-supplier relationships are reminiscent of the way in which U.S. auto manufacturers dealt with their suppliers under a mass production system rather than the way the Japanese (and now an increasing number of U.S. firms) deal with theirs to achieve lean production.

In a recent situation at AMS, we were developing a system using an application development environment supplied by a mid-sized West Coast software manufacturer.[19] They were working on a new release of their product, and we had been engaged in active (mostly electronic) discussions with them over key features. At some point it became clear that we just weren't making ourselves heard as to what the problems were likely to be, given certain changes they were proposing. We suggested, and they agreed, that it would be advantageous for some of our developers to visit their plant, existing applications in hand, to work with their engineers on an approach that would meet our needs (and likely those of a large number of their other customers) and still allow them to add the capabilities that their sales staff said were necessary to be competitive. A relatively small investment on our part resulted in a potentially enormous saving in rework that we would have had to do if the originally proposed changes had been implemented.

This was "lean production" in action and would have been unheard of just a few years ago. In this case, lean production worked because:

1. the software supplier was open with its customers about proposed new capabilities in its products (it trusted them).

2. we were open to spending some money up-front to work with the supplier, over and above the normal license and maintenance fees (we saw this as an investment in the relationship).

3. the supplier was open to joint work in their R&D environment, making their developers available to work with ours (they accepted the need for customers to be involved early in the process).

---

19. "Mid-sized" in the software business takes on a different meaning than in some other manufacturing industries; the 50th largest software manufacturer in the 1995 *Software Magazine* survey had $93 million in sales, while the 100th had only $30 million [Soft 1995]. By way of comparison, the 100th largest firm in the Fortune 500 was Compaq Computer with sales of almost $11 billion.

The essence of this approach sounds simple; implementing it requires a different way of thinking. You have to:

- work *with* your vendors rather than *over* your vendors: the master/slave form of relationship was discredited years ago, and it doesn't make sense when implementing information systems either. "Getting the best deal" no longer means getting the cheapest per copy price on your initial software or hardware license. It means a more cooperative process from the very beginning, including involving the vendor in the formulation of the basic requirements. Giving your vendors a chance to use their expertise for your benefit is one way to achieve synergy in the vendor-supplier relationship. A major auto manufacturer did this a few years ago and has since received over 9000 suggestions from vendors, of which over 6000 were implemented, resulting in almost $1 billion in savings so far.

- realize that the sooner you begin working together with suppliers, the better off you all will be. Waiting until the end of the procurement process (after all the specifications have been "frozen" and the RFP is ready to go out) to alert the vendors to your needs will hamper them and deprive you of the valuable insights that they can provide.

- look for partnerships with a *few* vendors rather than purchasing from many: only in this way do you have the critical mass to make the vendor part of the development process so that you can achieve the synergy that is possible when organizations work together. Yes, there is an element of "being locked in" but that is part of the risk you take to get a greater reward (and why it requires a greater commitment to understanding the vendor's organization and people).

- recognize that direct purchase cost is only one factor in the full life-cycle cost of a product: when you make purchase decisions, you are making a capital decision (the purchase or the initial development) and an operating cost decision (on-going maintenance). The latter often swamps the former.

24.4   THE BOTTOM LINE

"Make vs. buy" decisions occur at many points in the information systems industry. They must be made by hardware component vendors and hardware system vendors. They must be made by software component vendors and software system vendors. And they must be made by every computer-using organization considering how to develop its next major information system.

Understanding the IS technology supply chain will be key to improving time to market, cost effectiveness, and customer satisfaction in implementing new business systems. As the auto industry now understands, learning how to maximize the effectiveness of your relationships with technology suppliers will help you achieve competitive advantage.

25 Selecting Components

Once the basic architecture of the system has been determined and major components defined, the next question is how to select specific components from among the usually wide array of similar components on the market. Are there really differences among the vendors of PCs (dozens of choices), operating systems (three or more choices), database management systems (at least seven choices of relational database systems), network protocols (at least three major choices), client/server development tools (dozens) and all the rest?[20] Of course, there are. But not all of them matter, and sorting out the ones that do from the ones that don't is the important step in the analysis.

The typical approach to making a choice among multiple products is to perform the following steps (although not necessarily in this order).

- Determine desirable features for the product category and desirable capabilities of the vendors (e.g., on-line customer support).
- Determine which features and capabilities are most important by ranking and assigning relative weights (to be used as multipliers in ranking products).

---

20. In 1991, I chaired a working group at AMS to select a cross-platform GUI development tool (i.e., a development tool that would automatically create GUIs that would run under Windows, OS/2, and UNIX based on only a single design and source) for use in creating several new products. At the time, we were almost overwhelmed by the three choices that were available to us. Recent surveys in *Client/Server Computing* and *Software Magazine* list over two dozen!

- Gather information on different products and assess the degree of feature availability.
- Gather information on the vendors and assess the degree of desired capabilities.
- Assign a numerical rating to the degree to which each vendor or product possesses the feature or capability.
- Rank products (including the vendor capabilities) based on multiplying the feature availability score by feature weight and summing.
- Select the one with the highest score.

I have seen innumerable selection decisions made in just this way. In fact, decisions are often made based on one vendor and product scoring 342 and another only 339 out of a maximum of 500, a difference that can have no meaning whatsoever in terms of which is the better product for the situation. There has to be a better way—and there is.

The task of investigating software or hardware components is often turned into a project unto itself and can take anywhere from one to six months.[21] If the type of product is familiar to your organization (i.e., you are already using some vendor's version of the product), projects at the shorter end of this range seem reasonable—at first glance. If the type of product you are selecting is new to your organization, longer-duration projects seem reasonable—at first glance. The problem in both cases is that the selection projects are often a waste of time. Although they usually arrive at reasonable answers, most such answers could have been found with much less time and effort. Except in those cases of extreme operating requirements (millions of transactions per day, etc.), and assuming you have eliminated decisions that fail the test of meeting absolute constraints, almost any selection is likely to be acceptable. Here's why.

---

21. There seems to be an inverse correlation between length of selection process and making the correct decision. I have even seen some processes that took over a year and never reached a conclusion—the choices available had changed several times before the selection process was declared "overtaken by events."

- If you already know the product category and are satisfied with the specific product you are already using, why are you selecting another?
- If you already know the product and aren't satisfied, what went wrong with your selection process the first time around (unless you take the approach outlined below), and why will this time be different?
- If you don't know the product, what makes you think the selection criteria you have established are any good, or that the weightings and rankings are sufficiently accurate to make a decision based on them?
- If you don't know the product, what makes you think you can learn about it from reading literature, talking with vendors, or even trying to do some trivial application?

The problem with selecting client/server software components is that each seems to do everything you want—if you read the vendor's literature or reports of end-user successes published in the trade press or perform simple test cases.[22] The missing features, limitations on capabilities, and failure modes don't show themselves until you try to develop that 500-window application, or run with 200 users, or connect more than a dozen servers, or try some other "industrial strength" tactic. It is very difficult to justify the cost of a selection process that performs these kinds of "tests" on more than one product.

The most important research you can do to select your client/server components is to talk *in detail* to people who are already using them. If the vendor can't come up with at least a few folks who are using the product in an environment very similar to

---

22. The IS trade press is generally quite good, and its reporters quite conscientious (although I have never been a reporter, I do write columns for a number of trade publications, so I am at least a little biased). However, the reality of the medium is that many success stories are suggested to the press by the vendors of the products involved, so of course they show the best side of those products. I've gotten many requests for "failure" stories from reporters trying to do a balanced job, but somehow or other I've never been able to find one, or at least someone who wanted to talk about one.

yours (along *all* major dimensions), you are better off staying away.[23]

The second most important thing you can do is to use the product yourself. Of course, lab experiments and pilot projects won't tell you what the problems will be when you try to scale up to implement that new strategic system, but they will give you some basic familiarity with how the product works—and with dealing with the vendor's customer support organization.

So, here's how to select among different component vendors with minimum expenditure of time and money and maximum likelihood of finding the right product for your organization (several of the steps listed can be done simultaneously).

- *Start by looking at the vendor whose product is the most well known, is the acknowledged market leader, or is recommended by someone already using it in production.*[24] Making this determination requires talking with colleagues in other companies, meeting with industry analysts, going to industry meetings, and reading the trade press. You could just start with the vendor that has gotten the most press, but that may be a little less reliable. (I know I said— in a footnote—that much of this press is self-induced, or at least self-suggested, but even that requires having a reasonably good product and track record.) I assume your team has been doing their general reading and has seen most of the articles about the product they are researching, or can do an on-line search among the various databases now available to gather that information.
- *Investigate the vendor's financial situation.* If it is a public company, so much the easier, but don't hesitate to ask for,

---

23. This point, of course, does not apply to those of you who want to be in the 3 percent of people on the far left of the technology adoption curve (Figure 3 on page 27)—in which case you shouldn't be engaged in a long selection process anyway.

24. Some people might call this a truly Neanderthal approach, since, if everyone followed it religiously, it would mean that no new company or product would ever have a chance. Luckily for most of us, there are always some of us who are willing to try anything from anybody—a few of which products will actually turn out to be really good from companies that will continue to thrive—before the rest of us have to make up our minds. See [Grochow 1993] for more comments on this problem.

information from those that are privately held. It is almost impossible to predict which companies are going to be in business five years from now, let alone the twenty that your new system is supposed to last, but you better do as much homework as you possibly can.[25]

- *Start using the product.* Until you start installing it, creating an application around it, incorporating it into already running applications (by substituting it for some other component), you won't really have a feel for what it is like to use, or to deal with the vendor's customer support, a key selection criterion. In general, the cost of doing a pilot project will be a small part of your total commitment to the product.

- *Contact current users.* Visiting them is a good idea, particularly if the type of product is one that makes it a critical component of your system. Find out how others are really using the product. Are they still testing, or is it in production? If it is in production, is it with 10 users or 10,000? You find that you have to ask a lot of questions to sort this out, but my experience is that most of us like to talk with others about what we are doing, particularly if we get some good feedback in return.

- *Talk with the vendor's customer support people.* Are they knowledgeable beyond the first few chapters of the manual, and do they answer their phones and e-mail?

- If the product installs correctly (it is surprising how many do not), works with its own supplied test applications as well as some of your own, has no known incompatibilities with other components you plan on using (ask the vendor and check online databases), and passes the "current user" test, *go for it.*

Continue your relationship with the vendor even after you have made your purchase (*especially* after you have made your purchase!). As we have already discussed, maintaining on-going

---

25. There are so many counterexamples to this point that I hesitated to make it (just look at IBM and the slogan "You never get fired for selecting IBM"), but I still believe that significant "due diligence" is called for.

vendor relationships will be important to ironing out the inevitable difficulties that you will have later on. And, if you really hit a brick wall, you are much more likely to get the vendor to supply you with a "work around" to keep you in the fold rather than jumping ship to another vendor.

For established product categories such as operating systems, database management systems, and several others, there may or may not be significant differences among vendors. Aside from basic compatibility issues (does this particular product work with products in other component categories that you intend to use, e.g., the operating systems and network protocols?), it is often hard to distinguish among them. You will find equally zealous users of most database management systems, all sure that the vendor they use has the best product. If you did a side-by-side feature comparison, however, you would find at least an 85 percent overlap at any particular point in time, with the leadership shifting from vendor to vendor as each comes out with new releases and add-ons.

Selecting the right components and component vendors is an important step in building a successful system. It is made even more important due to the "lock in" effect that often occurs—in spite of industry movement to open systems. Whether it is inertia or trying to capitalize on an already-existing relationship, once you develop a strategic application using the products of a particular vendor, you are highly likely to build other systems using that vendor's products. As a result, we have become almost paranoid about how we make component selection decisions and tend to over-analyze most such situations. The point is that our resources are often better spent in working with one or two products and vendors than in attempting to study the field. Even then, our primary focus should be on the vendor since the features a product has today will be less important than the support the vendor gives tomorrow. This is the time-and-cost-efficient way to select component vendors.

26 A Workable Component Reuse Strategy

> **"**
> _____
>
> *Don't create, reuse.*
> _____
>
> **"**

This simple litany has been at the core of hundreds of attempts at improving system development productivity at levels unattainable by simple improvements in languages, tools, and procedures. While some organizations have achieved enviable productivity increases by implementing highly structured reuse programs (see, for example, [Tracz 1988] and [Grady 1987]), the large majority have not. Organizations that routinely buy software packages for processing their payrolls (the "ultimate" in reuse) have not even the most rudimentary program in place for reusing designs and code they write themselves. Given the cost of designing and writing that code (variously estimated at $10 to $100 per line), it would appear that there are significant benefits to be gained by using that code over and over again in multiple systems. But perhaps this logic isn't so logical, for why else has our industry had such difficulty in establishing a consistent and high level of reuse?

The reason is that *reuse isn't free*. Organizing to encourage reuse is often seen as an overwhelming task with an uncertain payback. A significant investment is required to create an organizational culture and environment complete with measurements and rewards for reuse (both for making "things" that are reusable and for reusing things already made), to set up a reuse library and staff it with active librarians (someone has to ensure that the stuff works—and continues to do so over time), and to create all the appropriate processes and procedures so that everything meshes. And there are more examples of companies that haven't gotten a sufficient return on this investment than those who have.[26]

One of our problems is that we try too hard to change the way people think rather than looking for incremental improvements in behavior without worrying about changing basic cultural paradigms.[27] If we can change the way they act, do we really need to win their hearts and minds first?

More and more organizations do seem to be getting serious about capitalizing on their software assets as well as recognizing that those assets extend far beyond the actual program code. Reusing code saves only a fraction of the total system cost.[28] Organizations can and should be reusing everything from methods to architectures to document formats to procedures to test plans. And many are now doing just that.

In one of many articles on the subject, Graham lists the key prerequisites to successful reuse [Graham 1995]:

- senior management understanding and support;
- realistic estimates of the investment required;
- a life-cycle model that incorporates reuse;

---

26. Besides, you'd have to be a certified masochist to want to go through all that trouble when you've got all those really great programmers sitting out there just waiting to create new programs to do the same thing that others have done a hundred times before—but, of course, better.

27. Well, I finally used *paradigm*, the "p" word. There is hardly a computer science book published these days that doesn't talk about changing the paradigm at least a dozen times. It's a fine word, just overused in the last few years as we try to move from one model (i.e., paradigm) of system development and implementation to another.

28. Suppose you purchased 50% of the actual code you need for a system. What kind of savings could you expect: 15%–20% by eliminating program design and coding, 10%–15% by reducing testing time, add back 5% for increased integration and vendor relationships, yields 20%–30% total savings on a 50% code reduction. If you purchase 100% of the code, i.e., a complete software package, you "max out" at 50%–60% overall savings, since you still have to do basic analysis, design, integration with other systems, acceptance testing, and a variety of implementation tasks.

- a library of reusable components and functions;
- a means of documenting and accessing these components via their specification;
- tools to facilitate this approach;
- a system that rewards for reuse; and
- the all-important skilled, motivated developers.

This list is mostly a general formula for success in introducing almost any new aspect of information systems technology. If we had them all, reuse wouldn't be a problem, and everyone would be doing it rather than writing about it.

One more observation: programmer productivity studies over the years found anywhere from 10:1 to 100:1 differences in productivity (i.e., amount of code delivered) from the worst to the best practitioner. This level of difference is not easily explainable by differences in industriousness, intelligence quotient, or raw native ability. There has to be something else. And there is. It is called reuse. The best programmers are the ones with the biggest filing cabinets, the largest number of friends, the most active correspondents, the largest list of magazines read, etc. In short, the high-productivity programmers are the ones who rarely design or write something from scratch. These people are constantly reusing things—code from their own lifetime libraries, designs given to them by others they have consulted with, ideas that show up in articles in magazines, books, etc. It isn't hard to imagine that this is the case—I have seen it, you've seen it, we do it ourselves.[29]

So here is my prescription: give all your developers the logical equivalent of a good filing cabinet of designs, program code, test plans, and the other components of the software engineering

---

29. In 1995, I wanted to demonstrate the latest interactive capabilities of the World Wide Web via Netscape's new JavaScript programming language. I read the manual (such as it was) on Netscape's site on the Internet (http://www.netscape.com) and found several coding examples, including a simple calculator. After making some basic modifications (such as putting in a "clear" key) just to prove to myself that I knew what I was doing, I put this "new" program on my Web page. I showed it to several of our developers, who were, somewhat to my bemusement, amazed that I could have developed such a "state of the art" application in so little time. Without reuse, I might still be working on it.

profession. Since most people need help in arranging their files and then in retrieving things, this "logical filing cabinet" has to have both a physical filing cabinet and a person to help arrange and retrieve the files (a "reuse librarian"). The physical filing cabinet should preferably be computerized, for example via Lotus's Notes. The person should be someone with a strong understanding of the system development process (probably a person who has already distinguished himself or herself in development management positions). Populate the filing cabinet with design documents, components of program code, sample GUI windows, test plans, projects plans—anything that you think has the least possibility of being useful to someone else— all in "as is" condition.[30] What you are really doing is creating a library of examples, showing people what has been done before that might be of use in the future—exactly what a reuse program is supposed to do.

One of the biggest problems in formal reuse programs is keeping library contents up-to-date, but why bother? Most people who consult a library are looking for something that they can paraphrase, excerpt, or use as a guide, not necessarily something that they can plagiarize verbatim. In the case of software, if the component is big enough to be purchased from a third-party vendor, it probably will be incorporated whole, as it should be, since you are paying the vendor to keep it working and up-to-date. But we aren't really talking about populating our reuse libraries with that kind of component (e.g., database management systems, generalized inquiry software, other middleware), but with the hundreds of other smaller software components and non-software components that might be useful in constructing strategic systems.

The reuse librarian in my prescription is a key ingredient to a successful reuse program. It is unfortunate that you can't count on people to refer to the library all the times that they should. After all, you haven't necessarily won over their hearts and

---

30. If you have some extra time and money, generalize some of those designs into standard-form design patterns and some of that code into generalized frameworks, but don't hold up implementing the basic strategy by waiting to take this step.

minds to reuse—you are just trying to change their behavior. And what better way to do it than by having a helpful librarian backed up by a substantial library at their beck and call?

If you want to go beyond the examples library approach to reuse, you can of course attempt to implement a more complete program based on the approach of Graham [1995] or Grady and Caswell [Grady 1987]. Don't ignore the examples library approach just because it appears simple; it is time tested and inexpensive, and it works.[31]

---

31. My colleagues Suzanne Cooper, Susan Hanley, and Janet McCabe at AMS get the credit for convincing me that this approach is far more time and cost effective than almost anything else one could do in the reuse arena, short of cultural-change brain implants for all system developers.

27 Open Issues in the Component Construction Approach to Development

> ❝
>
> *You're going to see a large revolution in the way products are architected—out of component objects that can be sold separately or built up to more complex products by other vendors or by end-users. It will be a pretty big step for the industry—it's not going to set in overnight—but that's the direction we're all heading for.*
>
> John Landry, chief technology officer, Lotus Development Corporation (now a part of IBM), quoted in [Semich 1995]
>
> ❞

If we combine the themes discussed in this chapter, we can see how the software development business has been changing over the past dozen or so years. Very few people still active in the business claim to write new systems completely from scratch—everybody is using at least some code that has seen service somewhere else.[32] Very few people would argue that developing a few very large (and inherently complex) programs is better than developing a large number

---

32. It is not necessarily the case that code has to change hands to be reused. Some of the most productive programmers I know are the ones who reuse their own code over and over. It would have been interesting to see if those studies that showed programmer productivity differences of up to 100 to 1 also showed that the best programmers had file cabinets (or hard disk drives) that were 100 times larger than the others. I'm convinced there is a strong correlation between productivity and the ability of the developer to maintain an active file of "previously owned" programs.

of simpler programs, that is, building systems with a highly modular structure. Very few would argue that licensing software products "may be OK for small organizations but it would never work in ours." In short, we have accepted the "component approach to development."

But component construction techniques are still in their relative infancy. We are still struggling with issues such as these.

- *What is the right number and size of components for optimal trade-offs of construction and maintenance complexity?*

  It is possible today to buy a "component" ranging in size from a few object classes comprising several hundred lines of code (e.g., routines to interface from Smalltalk to relational databases) to thousands of sub-routines comprising almost a million lines of code (e.g., the Open Software Foundation's Distributed Computing Environment). If we include application packages as components, the high end is even higher. The future is clearly bigger and bigger components because they provide more functionality with a smaller increase in system-level complexity.

- *How do we specify and then validate what components are supposed to do?*

  Component assemblers in industries such as automobile manufacturing are able to work with thousands of suppliers because they have learned how to create specifications, measures, and tests that can be understood and used by supplier and assembler alike. We do not have those in the software industry to any significant degree.[33]

- *Are interface standards sufficiently robust to allow ready substitution of supposedly compatible components?*

  Interface standards are fraught with complexities and ambiguities. Even in something as long-lived as the TCP/IP networking protocol, we have to deal with incompatibilities among software vendors who all claim to follow the

---

33. Chapter 24 *The Component Approach Creates an IS Technology Supply Chain* on page 160 discusses issues created by having to deal with a large number of component vendors in constructing systems.

standards. When it comes to more complex or less mature issues, such as distributed object request brokers (communicating at the object level across a network), interface specifications vary significantly among standards proposed by different parties.[34]

- *Will there really be a thriving component industry with long-lived suppliers?*

  Many component vendors are small "garage shops" with no long-term history of support, new releases, or even survival. In fact, there is some question as to whether the currently accepted licensing mechanisms are sufficient to allow all but the largest component manufacturers to develop a profitable business. Licensing mechanisms that do not take account of the multiple types and levels of reuse of a component may not allow the initial developer to derive enough revenues to support the base product.[35]

Some fairly basic and thorny issues about component construction techniques have yet to be resolved. Although this hasn't stopped the increasing use of components, it has certainly limited large-scale acceptance and the growth of the component software industry. The economic implications are sufficiently large, however, as to make this author confident that acceptable (although certainly not perfect) solutions will be forthcoming.

---

34. In the case of distributed ORBs, developers can only hope that Microsoft and the rest of the industry converges on a single standard, but more likely there will be two standards to deal with: the Object Management Group's Common Object Request Broker Architecture and Microsoft's Distributed OLE.

35. [Cox 1992] suggests an innovative approach to this problem that is being actively researched in Japan: monitoring the use of components via hardware incorporated into every computer sold and reporting that usage automatically via modem. It makes for interesting reading, but I am somewhat skeptical that his scheme will ever be generally adopted (although we are already seeing specialized cases where something like this has been tried on a relatively small scale). [Brad Cox is a colorful writer with many broad-based concerns. In the same article, he discusses the problem newspaper publishers are having in figuring out electronic distribution and payment issues: "Nearly half of our bulk-waste problem would be eliminated if we could break the habit of fondling the macerated remains of some forest critter's home as we drink our morning coffee."]

Connecting the Components: Client/Server and Object Technology

Over the past several years, there has been a growing consensus (one might say it has reached the stage of "widespread agreement") that client/server technology provides the most powerful way of delivering computing resources to end-users. There is somewhat less agreement, however, on the best approach to implementing client/server systems. As an industry, we are still trying to answer the question "What development technology will enable us to implement the most efficient, robust, and maintainable client/server applications?" There is a growing consensus (almost at the widespread-agreement level) that object technology provides the answer.

> *...our Distributed Connection Object allows you to create sophisticated client/server applications...*
>
> paraphrased from the marketing brochures of any number of middleware vendors

28 Implementing Client/Server Systems with Objects

Material in this section is adapted from [Grochow 1994].

Client/server systems can be implemented using a variety of development tools, techniques, and methods. You can use structured techniques and implement in COBOL (brought into the client/server world with appropriate add-ons and run-time additions). You can use almost any methodology and CASE tools that have been expanded to split the application between client and server, such as Intersolv's APS or Seer's HPS.[1] You can use rapid application development strategies and one of the dozen or so new 4GLs specifically designed for the client/server environment, for example, Forte, Powerbuilder, Progress, or SQL Windows.[2] You can even use one of the 4GLs that have served us well in the mainframe database arena, extended to allow parts of the application to reside on client machines and parts on servers. And, of course, you can use object methods and object languages and tools.

In the good old days of the 1980s, we didn't have to deal with the alternatives just listed: we developed our systems in COBOL (I'm talking about business systems, of course) or maybe a 4GL that we got from our database vendor (Ada-

---

1. Of course you wouldn't call them CASE tools anymore. Not that "computer-aided software engineering" isn't what we are trying to do, but rather that CASE per se received so much hype at its introduction over a decade ago, and then so much bad publicity for not delivering the goods, that it currently is out of vogue. It is interesting that all the vendors that used to produce "software development tools" then produced "CASE tools" and now produce "object-oriented client/server application development environments"—usually by extending the same initial products.

2. More than a few organizations are taking this approach. IDC estimates, for example, that the client/server 4GL market was more than $2 billion in 1995.

bas's NATURAL comes to mind). Now, not only do we have to implement the best system, but we have to choose the best development strategy and tools as well. Figure 53 lists some of the pros and cons of each stratedy

Figure 53: C/S implementation environments

Environment	Example	Pros	Cons
COBOL	Microfocus	Lots of people know the language	Requires add-ons to provide GUI, C/S, considered "old fashioned"
New 4GL	Forte, Powerbuilder, Progress, SQL Windows	Designed for C/S environment	Little experience with long-term maintainability or stability of vendors
Existing 4GLs	NATURAL	Proven usefulness	Extensions for C/S may not be as robust as in new 4GLs
New CASE tool	HPS	Designed for C/S environment	Little experience with long-term maintainability, or stability of vendors
Existing CASE tool	APS	Proven usefulness, long-term viability of vendors	Extensions for C/S may not be as robust as in newer tools
Object Language	Smalltalk, C + +	Benefits of object technology	Little experience with long-term maintainability, new approach, stability of vendors

Object technology will be the long-term solution for client/server systems. It provides the conceptual approach for building frameworks and components that are the unit of distribution for distributed applications. When you change your mind about where functions should reside (which you will), the objects that implement them won't have to be modified since the message-handling facility (the "object request broker," or ORB) will keep communication flowing. The implementation of compatible

ORBs from multiple vendors (HP, IBM, Iona, Sun, and others) based on the Object Management Group's CORBA standard will allow objects to communicate across heterogeneous platforms and languages. You can even "wrapper" existing programs or systems by defining them as objects via the Interface Definition Language provided with these ORBs. In other words, *any* program, whether implemented in an object language or a 3GL or a 4GL, will be able to use the object message passing approach to achieve a level of module encapsulation unavailable up to now. And this is the key to flexible client/server implementations.

This level of flexibility cannot be achieved effectively with any of the alternatives to object technology. Take, for example, 3GL applications written in C or COBOL. Components communicate via sub-routine calls, and that is proving problematic in creating client/server applications for heterogeneous environments. A key component of this development strategy is the remote procedure call (RPC) library, which typically implements a large number of complex APIs that the programmer must master.[3] This complexity and the associated learning curve mean that it takes a lot of work to move a part of the application to a remote system. The middleware solutions to this problem usually solve it by limiting the functionality available to the programmer. The desire to make this type of environment viable is one of the reasons the middleware market is booming.

Proprietary 4GLs also begin with a strike against them: by definition they are proprietary. While some are now beginning to provide robust capabilities for defining which parts of the application reside on the client and which on the server, these mechanisms are also proprietary to the particular 4GL tool being used. This means that you become totally dependent on a single vendor for determining which platforms you can communicate with, which network protocols you can use, and, more impor-

---

3. RPC is the expansion of the sub-routine concept to client/server environments. It provides the infrastructure to deal with finding out where the called sub-routine is supposed to be (on what network, on what computer), determining whether that computer is available, sending calling parameters over the network, and dealing with errors and error recovery. Needless to say, it is somewhat more complex to do a remote procedure call than a local procedure call.

tant, which components you can have on which platform (so much for "open systems").

This is not to say that these problems will not be solved in time and that 3GL and 4GL vendors will not start to incorporate standard "open" approaches into their products. They will, and when they do, they will be using the same ORBs available now in the object world—in effect, 3GL and 4GL environments will have become part of the object environment.

CONNECTIONS: *Objects and Client/Server*

If the question is "what technology will provide the most efficient, robust, and maintainable client/server environment" today, the only answer is object technology. Tomorrow, the only answer will be object technology as well, but we'll have a lot more compatible choices to pick from.

29 The Future of Client/Server: Distributed Object Computing

Having said that client/server systems increasingly will be implemented using objects, it is necessary to discuss the several ways in which that can be done. For some very practical reasons having to do with the availability of infrastructure software, these can be thought of as progressive "stages of distributed object computing," progressing from a traditional non-object world to a world consisting completely of objects.

In the first stage (see Figure 54), an object-oriented system is created but needs to communicate with a relationship database. In this typical two-tier client/server system, all of the objects are on a single machine, and the database server employs traditional technology. The middleware that does the object-to-relational transformation resides on the same machine as the application so that the database server is ignorant of the fact that the application is implemented using objects.

Figure 55 shows a more complex client/server system, but again with all the objects residing on one machine. In this case, the object application is communicating with a legacy system and its database residing on the mainframe. The object-legacy communications is similar conceptually to the inter-machine communications in the previous example, although arguably more difficult to implement. In this type of multi-tier client/server system, the application function will typically be split between mainframe and end-user computers, although sometimes only the user interface programming will be resident on the end-user computer.

192

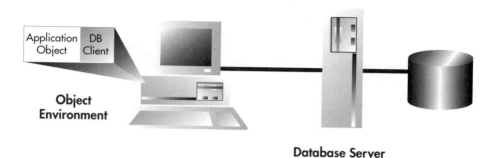

Figure 54: Distributed object computing—stage 1

Figure 55: Distributed computing—stage 2

The third-stage in distributed object computing introduces cross-machine logical object-to-object communication. Figure 56 shows an object application on one computer communicating with an object system on another computer, as well as with a legacy application and a database server (although not all three types of communication need be present). This will require more robust middleware to handle both object and non-object communication.

In third-stage systems, an application object on one computer would send its message explicitly to a communications object (as shown in the diagram), which would link with appropriate communication middleware (in the case shown, the Distributed

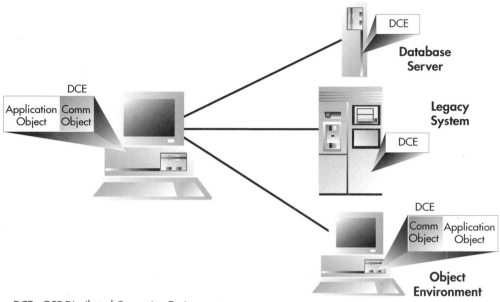

DCE= OSF Distributed Computing Environment

Figure 56: Distributed computing—stage 3

Computing Environment).[4] The middleware would communicate with similar middleware on other computers. If the application object were communicating with a legacy system or database server, appropriate programs on these computers would communicate back with the communications middleware. If the application object were communicating with another object application, then the communication middleware would similarly link with a communication object, which would communicate with the corresponding application object. In this case, an application object on one computer is sending messages to an application object on another computer via helper objects, but the communication mechanism is not an object-oriented mechanism.

---

4. The diagram indicates the Distributed Computing Environment as the communication middleware, but any appropriate communication mechanism could be used.

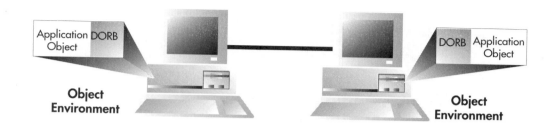

DORB = Distributed Object Request Broker

Figure 57: Distributed computing—stage 4

Finally, in the fourth stage (Figure 57), we truly have "distributed objects," that is, objects exchanging messages with other objects that are on different computers. An object on one computer sends a message as it would to any object. The object on the other computer receives that message as it would have any other object. Communications are handled transparently to the sending and receiving objects by a "distributed object request broker," middleware available from at least a dozen major and not-so-major vendors [Hayes 1995].

Although stage four provides true distributed object computing, it is not necessary to go directly to stage four to have success with objects and client/server. Each stage can be shown to provide a valuable approach to implementing client/server systems that will add value to their organizations. Each can also be shown to have technical advantages and disadvantages, most often related to the specific middleware products being used and the limitations they place on hardware, software, and network platforms.[5] Making the appropriate trade-off between distributed functionality, flexibility, and cost is, of course, part of the art of developing valuable systems.

---

5. For those of you "rolling your own" distributed object request brokers, there is, of course, even greater variability in advantages and disadvantages. The real "innovators," the organizations implementing stage four systems several years ago, had to implement their own— the commercial market had nothing viable. This situation has changed rather dramatically, and it is not unusual to have four or more DORBs to choose from.

I terative and Incremental Development

> ❝
>
> *The 'get it right the first time'*
> *philosophy in software engineering is*
> *astonishing and radically at odds with*
> *other forms of engineering. Regular*
> *cycles of trial and test are an integral*
> *part of the development process in the*
> *manufacture of automobiles, boats,*
> *airplanes, factory machinery, and*
> *coffee makers. No one dreams that*
> *they can go from design to finished*
> *product without test and revision.*
> *How the contrary arrogance has*
> *gotten imbedded in software*
> *development is a mystery.*
>
> Thomas K. Landauer, in [Landauer 1995], p. 173)
>
> ❞

30 Problems with Waterfalls Lead to Spirals

Several models of the system life-cycle have been used to describe the ways in which system development projects proceed from initiation through implementation: "waterfall," "spiral," iterative, incremental.[1] The basic difference among the models has to do with perceived completeness and feedback among the various steps: is each step in the life-cycle "completed" before moving on to the next? Does information from one part of the life-cycle feed back to a previous part of the life-cycle?

The oft-referred-to waterfall model outlines a process where each stage is basically completed before moving on to the next, although feedback to a single prior stage is recognized.[2] The iterative model, however, assumes that system development is not a linear process and that developers plan on a series of iterations, both within stages and across stages. The incremental model assumes that system functions cannot be specified completely at the beginning of a project and that a learning process has to take place as some portion of the system (an increment) is developed.

In fact, many developers have recognized the waterfall as simply an imperfect model of a much more complicated development process. A

---

1. The spiral model described by Boehm is an attempt to encompass all the others [Boehm 1988].

2. Most discussions of the waterfall assume that the steps are followed in a strictly linear stage-by-stage fashion—as in "it's tough to move back up a waterfall." Boehm calls this strictly linear approach the "stagewise" model, a term that has not achieved widespread use. He specifically notes the inclusion of feedback from one step to another as the key enhancement that the waterfall model brings over the stagewise model.

study done at the Microelectronics and Computer Technology Corporation (MCC) shows what really happens when analysts and programmers work: there is an almost constant shifting back and forth among high-level and detailed activities (as shown in Figure 58 from [Yourdon 1989]). In attempting to validate a high-level concept, it may be necessary to engage in a detailed prototype. In attempting to implement a detailed program specification, it may be useful to review (or perhaps modify) a higher-level design or concept. These microsteps in the development process never show up in any task plan because they are not planned—they just happen in the "normal" process of accomplishing the larger tasks.

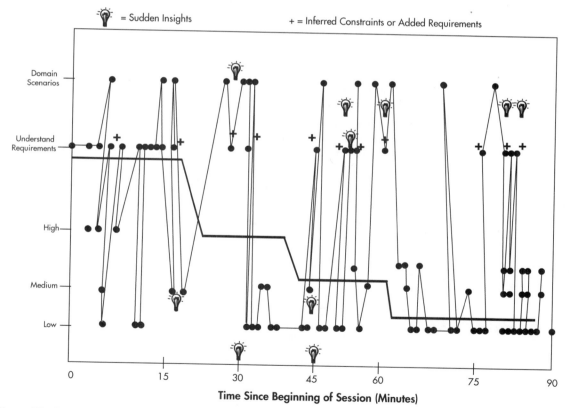

Figure 58: Empirical analysis of software development

Many methodologies have been based on the stagewise and waterfall models, and many systems have been developed using a more-or-less linear systems development strategy. In general, it was easier to plan and manage a linear life-cycle (versus one that included lots of feedback loops and iteration), and that led to the illusion that such approaches led to the best systems. Unfortunately, the amount of rework and "perfective maintenance" required by most systems developed under a waterfall approach would seem to invalidate this assumption. As stated very well in [Somogyi 1987]:

> *First, the linear view of the life-cycle can be misleading. Systems developed in a linear fashion were built on the premise that successive deductions would be made during the development process, each such deductive step supplying a more detailed specification to the next one. As no recursive action was allowed, the misconceptions, errors and omissions left in by an earlier step would result in an ever-increasing number of errors and faults being built into the final system...*

> *Second, there are problems associated with specifications. The linear life-cycle view also assumed that a system could be safely built for a long life, once a specification had been correctly developed, as adjustments were unlikely to be required provided the specification was followed attentively. This view had negated the possibility that systems might have a changing effect on their environment, which, in turn, would raise the requirement for tuning and readjusting them. The followers of this approach had also overlooked the fact that real business, which these systems were supposed to serve, never remains constant. It changes, thereby changing the original requirements. This, in turn, would require re-adjusting or even scrapping the system. Furthermore, the idea that users could specify precisely their requirements seems to have been largely a fallacy, negating the basis on which quite a few systems had been built.*

So, here we have all the problems of linear system development approaches stated at once:

- Misconceptions and errors are propagated from one phase to the next one.

- Once implemented, systems have an effect on their environment that generates the need for changes to the system.
- The business supported by the system itself changes during the course of the system's life.
- End-users are not able to precisely state their "requirements" during the initial stages of system design (or perhaps ever).[3]

If ever there were a specification for a new approach to system development, here it is. We need a system development model that:

- allows the opportunity to correct misconceptions and errors introduced during earlier stages of the process;
- allows implementation of the system in phases to see what effects each has on the end-user environment;
- includes multiple opportunities to update the system as the business environment changes; and
- allows for the fact that users cannot be expected to state precisely their requirements and that the system will have to be updated as these requirements become clearer.

The spiral model described by Boehm is an empirically determined response to these specifications. It shows system development as a series of stages of design–prototype–validate leading to increasingly complete prototypes and eventually to a waterfall-like design–code–test cycle for the operational system. This model includes iteration, incremental development, and waterfall development. Much of the popular press ignores the richness of the spiral model, however, and incremental and iter-

---

3. We all know that it is dangerous to rely on the end-user "requirements" stated to the analyst in the early stages of design. (I discuss this further in Section 32.1 *An Aside About "Requirements"* on page 211. For now, however, I use this term for its common meaning.) Perhaps there was a time when we did have the belief that specifications could be exactly determined in interviews with prospective end-users. We certainly acted as if these specifications were exact: we "froze" the design so we could get on with the coding. Of course, we then spent the first six months (if not more) of system operation making "enhancements" that were really just corrections to the specifications. We knew all along that getting precise user specifications was a myth that we went along with in order to get a signoff on our work.

ative development are portrayed as something quite different. In fact, *any* approach to system development can be described as a subset of the spiral model.

Figure 59 (from [Boehm 1988]) shows the spiral model in all its glory. Begin at the center of the spiral with "requirements" and a "life-cycle plan." Go through a cycle of risk analysis, prototype, and concept. Continue to the next level of the spiral and perform a cycle of risk analysis, prototype, software requirements, requirements validation, and development plan. Each iterative cycle brings you closer to the "operational prototype" (on the outermost spiral). In Boehm's analysis, this prototype has allowed you to finally understand the system enough to proceed with detailed design, coding, and testing of the production system. Even then, you have only created "phase one" (the first system "increment") and should continue through another cycle to develop one or more functionally richer system increments or phases.

Coming back to the waterfall model, we have mostly realized that it does not work in the strict sense, but it can be made to work in a general sense—and that is what we have been doing for the past several decades. Implementation using the new information systems technology, however, *allows* us to use iterative and incremental approaches more effectively to develop systems that are more effective. The assumption is that incremental and iterative development result in better systems at lower cost, something that we have a great deal of anecdotal evidence on and only now are beginning to quantify.[4]

So, for the purposes of understanding how best to develop systems using the new information systems technology, the spiral says it all. More and more strategic systems projects are knowingly or unknowingly taking this approach.

---

4. I distinguish the costs and benefits of using these development approaches from the costs and benefits of implementing client/server systems, which recent studies have shown to be more expensive than comparable mainframe-based systems. If we can harness the power of the incremental and iterative approaches to arrive at good systems that meet users' needs, then we will save money *on the development approach*. Whether we are talking about mainframe (old technology) or client/server (new technology), we still need a development approach that will let us define what the system needs to do and then make it do that.

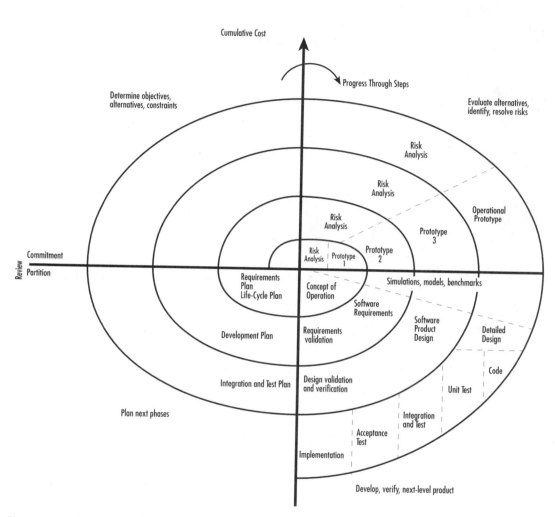

Figure 59: Spiral model of system development

31 Iterating and Incrementing

Iterative and incremental techniques can (and should) be used in developing systems that are expected to have high value to the organization. Dealing with the uncertainties of changing business processes and using new technology requires the flexibility inherent in these approaches.[5]

Iteration in the system development life-cycle can occur within a particular stage as well as across stages. The basis of this technique is the

---

5. Although "flexibility" should not imply "sloppy" or "incomplete" or "half-baked," as I discuss in Chapter 32 *How Do You Keep Things Under Control When You Are Iterating and Incrementing?* on page 209

assumption that system functions cannot be specified completely without interaction between end-user, designer, and prototypes of the system. If you are involved in designing the user interface, for example, you will produce a prototype that you think represents what the system should do. After exploring that prototype with the end-users, you will undoubtedly revise it, perhaps changing some features, adding or deleting others. In this way, you iterate toward the final product, that is the finished user interface design.

Figure 60 depicts analysis, design, prototype, and construction activities in an iterative environment. This is, at best, a rough indication of the time sequencing in which these activities occur since multiple feedback loops between activities are the norm. Two increments are shown, although many more may be performed, with some being scheduled and formal while others are "sub-iterations" occurring within a formal iteration. One difficulty of planning and managing projects using iterative approaches is creating task plans and schedules that take proper account of the iterative nature of the process.

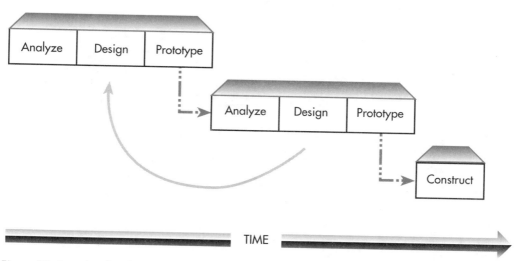

Figure 60: Iterative development

The incremental approach to systems development also assumes that system functions cannot be completely known at the beginning of a project and that it is desirable to implement a portion of the system (an increment) as quickly as possible. Multiple increments are planned, some expanding functionality in already implemented areas, and others adding new areas. In a loan processing system, the first increment might implement simple mortgage loans, for example. The second increment could add student loans and also mortgage refinancing. The third increment might deal with credit cards, while the fourth would go back and include other type of mortgages such as wraps and home equities. In this way, the organization gains the benefits of having parts of the system available sooner, end-users gain experience with the operation of the system, and designers get to see what frameworks and general system characteristics might need to be changed to improve its effectiveness—with an opportunity to do so in future increments. The benefits of the incremental approach are both the value gained from the use of initial increments and the value gained from improvements made to the entire system via subsequent increments.

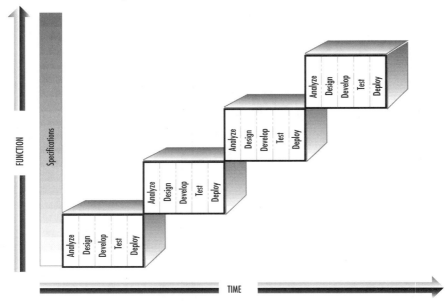

Figure 61: Incremental development

Figure 61 shows a system timeline for a project with four increments. In this depiction, high-level specifications are created for the full scope of the system and then broken down into the four increments to be developed. This is once again a highly stylized representation since there are myriad ways in which incremental development projects can be carried out in practice.

Figure 62 combines iterative and incremental approaches, showing the iterative approach being taken within each increment of system development. This diagram has the faults of both diagrams on which it is based. The full range of ways incremental and iterative techniques can be combined is yet to be explored and is limited only by our ability to control system development projects so that they produce the desired results in the desired time-frame for the desired cost. Unfortunately, in our zeal to effect these new ideas about systems development, we sometimes let projects get out of control, with the result that the value is lost—and that is what the next section is all about.

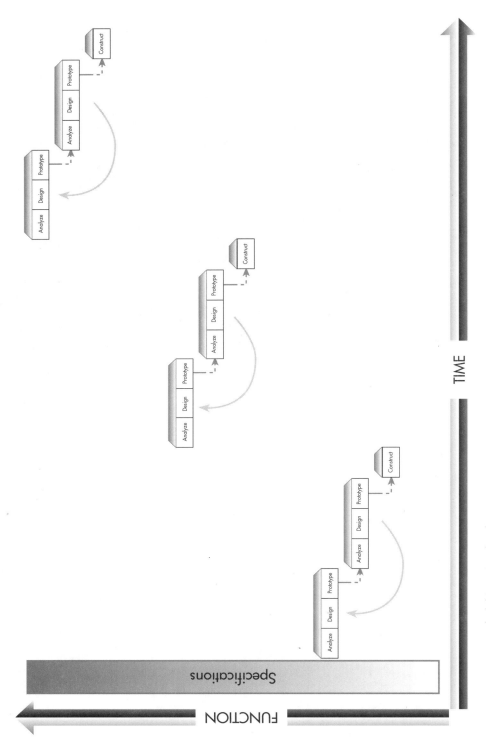

Figure 62: Incremental and iterative development

32 How Do You Keep Things Under Control When You Are Iterating and Incrementing?

In his book *Assessment and Control of Software Risks*, Capers Jones lists "creeping user requirements" as the number one risk in successfully implementing new management information systems.[6] It occurs in 80 percent of the thousands of projects in his database and averages 1 percent per month (see [Jones 1994a], p. 29). Elsewhere he cites creeping requirements as a triggering factor in detecting potential project disasters ([Jones 1995]).

The opposite of "requirements creep" is "requirements stability," and stable requirements means that we have identified all requirements at the beginning of the project. Time and experience have shown that this is an almost impossible task. This is exactly the issue that incremental and iterative development techniques are expected to solve. We cannot nail down a list of requirements during a so-called "requirements analysis phase" because those so-called requirements aren't even known to the end-users. We must, therefore, be prepared for shift and change in our understanding of system scope and features as we move through the development cycle—at least to a certain extent. But how then do we avoid the seeming dilemma of having to *control* system scope at the same

---

6. I question whether these developers ever really knew their "requirements" in the first place. See Section 32.1 *An Aside About "Requirements"* on page 211.

time that we are allowing system scope to evolve with our evolving understanding?[7]

The first thing to realize is that it is impossible to deliver a system without deciding at some point on a specific (i.e., fixed) set of functions and features. Iteration has to stop or you never have a finished product, which is, of course, what end-users really want. Incremental development has to result in an official "Release 1.0," a working system that has sufficient features and is sufficiently robust to be put into production. Some would say that incremental development actually continues forever as you produce Releases 2, 3, and 4 of the system—but there still has to be a Release 1.[8]

The key to delivering systems that are viewed as successful (i.e., that are accepted by their users, that are developed for the expected budget, and that are delivered more or less on the proposed schedule) is knowing when to stop iterating or to continue iterating, when to deliver an incremental release, or when to add more features. I wish I had a prescriptive approach to identifying these points, but I don't. This is where you have to rely on the skill and training of your senior project managers and analysts to make the call. There are several steps that you and they can take, however, to try to make the optimum stopping point more apparent.

- *Regardless of how much incrementing and iterating you plan on doing, divide the project into well-defined phases.*

One of the great fallacies of the incremental and iterative approaches to systems development is that it is somehow all

---

7. A good analogy came to me via the Requirement Engineering mailing list on the Internet: "when the rate of change of requirements starts to increase it is rather like heating up a solid…. slowly it loses shape, becomes liquid, and you end up with vaporware." [The Internet being a developing medium for interchange of ideas, the author of this analogy copyrighted it with reference to his home page at http://www.csci.csusb.edu/dick/ signature.html.]

8. Our industry already has a reputation that Release 1 of anything is still a test, that it isn't sufficiently feature-rich or operationally robust to warrant being put into production, but that the vendor had to release it anyway for marketing and financial reasons. In fact, there are some who say that it is actually Release 3.1 that is the first really usable release (remember Windows?). The cynics among us will note that at least one company was known to have labeled its first release "3.1" for just this reason.

right to begin coding before there is a design, to begin designing before there is sufficient analysis, or to deliver before there is sufficient testing. This is nonsense, and system failures abound to prove it.

- *Define "deliverables" for each person or team, tangible work products to be delivered in a specified time through each phase.*

A deliverables-based development cycle is less likely to get out of control because something tangible (memo, design document, compiled code, test plan, demonstration) always has to be shown as proof positive of progress rather than the typical "we're half-way there" type of progress report that is so often at the root of out-of-control projects.

- *Similarly, define "milestones," identifiable points where a progress review will be taken.*

Defining milestones may seem like one of the most antithetical things to do in an iterative development cycle, but of course, that is not the case. Somehow, we have to be able to decide whether the latest iteration or increment accomplished enough or whether another cycle is indicated. Often, an important step in ensuring that the project is under control is to establish a formal milestone at the end of an iteration period, so that someone else can take a look at how things are going.

The key to successfully adopting incremental and iterative techniques is to apply deliverable-based management with a level of flexibility that allows new information found during the process to filter into the overall system plan. You will learn important things during each of the phases of system development, and you must provide for that knowledge to be used. Your task in managing these "new information systems technology concepts" is to make sure that they are effectively blended with the other good ideas that our industry has learned over the past 25 years and that still make sense.

32.1 AN ASIDE ABOUT "REQUIREMENTS"

The literature of our discipline is rife with discussions of how to determine system requirements or user requirements. These are statements of the functions the system must perform (e.g., "the system must be able to list all receivables over 60 days old") or statements of the way they must be performed (e.g., "all user responses will be received in under five seconds"). Gause and Weinberg [Gause 1989] look at this as dividing the world into that which we want (requirements) and that which we don't want. If the system does what we want, it is successful. If it doesn't, it doesn't meet its requirements and it is a failure, or at least less than successful. Many practitioners are now measuring system quality in terms of how well the system meets user requirements.

Unfortunately, as we know now (most of us, anyway), requirements are very difficult to determine and, in fact, there may be far fewer "requirements" (i.e., things that the system must do) than most people realize. If the feature that the user says she absolutely has to have will add $1 million to the system development cost, will her supervisor agree that this particular feature is actually a "requirement"? In a few cases the answer will be "yes," but in many more cases the answer will be "no."

True requirements are not determined simply by asking end-users what features and functions they want to have in their new system. True requirements are actually determined as the endpoint of a larger process that includes this step (i.e., asking users what they want), but begins with a determination of overall objectives that the system is meant to satisfy. The "requirements determination process" thus begins to look like this.

1. Determine management objectives for the system (e.g., "help reduce receivables by five days"). This is most often accomplished by interviewing end-users and other "stakeholders."

2. Interview end-users to determine desired features and functions in support of the objectives. (This is the step that is typically, but erroneously, called "requirements gathering.")

3. Factor in knowledge of the subject area or domain to arrive at a complete list of functions.

4. Apply various constraints that management imposes on the system (e.g., "it cannot cost more than x dollars"), the

development environment (e.g., "it must use existing databases"), the operational environment (e.g., "the system must be usable by 90% of existing staff"), or the time to deliver (e.g. "the fiscal year begins on January 1").

Figure 63 represents pictorially the relationship of these tasks.

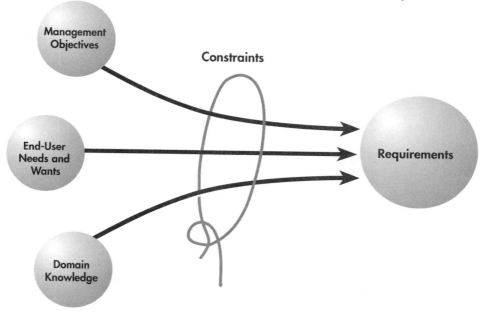

Figure 63: Requirements determination

We now have a new definition of "requirements."

A system requirement is a function or feature needed to support management objectives in a particular subject area (domain) that is not in violation of any management or environmental constraints.

This is far different than saying that requirements are simply what the end-users say they are. In fact, some practitioners go so far as to say "there is no such thing as 'user requirements'—we formulate *system* requirements based on a variety of factors—we don't gather requirements from users." Systems that satisfy system requirements that have been determined in this manner are the ones that create value for the organizations using them.

User Interface Technology

Interacting with computers has always been somewhat painful for the uninitiated. From the earliest computers with their punched-paper-tape input, to computers with typewriter input devices, to mainframes and personal computers with video screen text input, the "user interface" seemed always to be an afterthought. The back-seat role of the user interface designer (if there was one) would become a frontseat role, however, when PCs brought computing power to a much broader and certainly more diverse audience—and when practitioners began to realize that a computer system that would be easy to understand had a much higher value. With the advent of the Apple Macintosh in 1984, we entered the age of the "graphic user interface," and since then, it has been getting better all the time. There is no doubt that new advances in user interface technology will continue to increase the value of information systems long into the future.

33

Windows, Icons, Mice, and Pull-downs: The Graphic User Interface (GUI) ▼

Over 100 million people have experienced some version of the graphic user interface common to today's personal computers. While this may make it questionable whether graphic user interfaces are "new" information systems technology, it is interesting that it is almost impossible to explain GUI adequately in print, by discourse or diagrams, or even graphics.[1]

Figure 64 is a screen snapshot of my Windows 95® graphic user interface "desktop" as I worked on this book. While a picture may be worth some number of words, it hardly conveys the impact of what it is like to work with today's typical user interface. The ability of the author to create, revise, and edit is orders of magnitude greater than with simple textual interfaces of recent memory. The ability of the service representative to gain access to multiple sources of information while a customer is on the telephone has been similarly increased. And the ability of the previously non-computer-literate to approach the computer to do almost anything at all is greatly

---

1. This point actually raises a serious problem with creating user interface design documentation as well as end-user manuals. It is extremely difficult to document in written form all possible interactions among windows, mouse and text input, and system reactions. Even if you do manage to get all this put down in some reasonably coherent way, it is unlikely to convey the "look and feel" of the application, and that is what really makes a difference to the end-user. It is one of the reasons that creating working prototypes is an absolute necessity in the development of software using the new information systems technology. Of course, it still leaves the problem of providing end-user documentation, but more and more of that is being relegated to on-line information databases. No matter how little of the user manual you think today's computer user reads, tomorrow's will read even less—just ask my children who expect every function, button, pulldown list, and required mouse click to be totally self evident from what appears in front of them on the screen.

expanded. To truly understand why this is so, personal experience is the most effective teacher so, I won't belabor the point here.

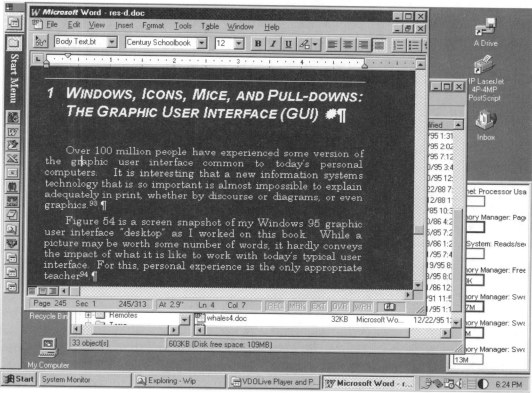

Figure 64: Graphic user interface example

34 Now We Add Audio and Video

Video and audio are relatively recent enhancements to the commonly available user interface. Both hardware and software to enable these capabilities have advanced rapidly in the past several years.

Hardware is no longer an impediment to more-sophisticated user interfaces. Today's typical PC configuration retailing in the $2000–3000 range includes capabilities for playing and recording reasonable quality audio (certainly for voice, although music quality can be added at extra expense). Most machines can now handle full-motion video viewing, and passable video recording can be added for as little as $100. Some machines come bundled with software to allow rudimentary voice commands to activate various programs.

With hundreds of megabytes of disk storage inexpensively available, as well as the almost-omnipresent CD-ROM, storing video content is less of a problem; and video clips are regularly included in all types of software, from games to tax preparation to business functions. In many cases, the video is used for training or providing substantive assistance to end-users as they do their jobs. For example, Boeing has an experimental aircraft repair system that not only lists the repair steps for each procedure but also shows via video a mechanic performing each step on an actual airplane. Other companies have incorporated audio and video into customer service systems to guide their representatives more directly in dealing with the ever-increasing variety of questions they must field.

Video content must still be created and then incorporated into software to be easily accessible. The introduction of the World Wide Web into business and commerce has dealt a swift blow to the complexity of incorporating video (and audio and graphics) into the user interface with its easy-to-understand programming in HTML. While high-quality video content requires the labor of skilled practitioners with expensive equipment, effectively using this video content is easy enough for most organizations (and many individuals) to handle. Just check out the World Wide Web to prove this to yourself.

Video and audio are more natural than text or even graphics to the vast majority of the population and are increasingly being used to support the business functions of systems. Systems incorporating these media are quickly becoming the norm, and we are beginning to wonder how we ever got along without them as part of the user interface.

35 What Next?

Many organizations are actively involved in research on future generations of user interface technology. This is much more than an academic pursuit, since there is significant money to be made in establishing the next standard and getting millions of people to adopt your approach. Several manufacturers are actively involving the broader public by producing videos showing their approaches and ideas. All are characterized by active use of multiple media—text, graphics, video, audio, speech recognition, etc.—and new devices for both input and output. The human-computer interface technology of the future will be multi-dimensional in much the same way that human-human interface technology is today.

To get a glimpse of the future, you can look at the highly publicized efforts of Microsoft, Apple, and AT&T, among others. AT&T turned their efforts into a national television advertising campaign called "Connections" that focused on highly portable computer devices that could be taken anywhere and communicate with anything or anybody. Microsoft has distributed thousands of copies of their "Information at Your Fingertips" video showing how computer and communications technology will be incorporated into everyday devices to provide information when you need it. Both of these examples showcase the use of "intelligent agents," software that learns about your needs and helps you to accomplish your tasks (see the following section). These videos are readily available from their producers and should help you in generating ideas and visualizing the future of your own user interfaces.

Microsoft and others are working on projects related to new types of user interfaces called "social" interfaces. This technology employs direct speech and animated graphics in an attempt to give end-users the impression that they are communicating with a smart personal assistant rather than a computer. While this type of interface has been a staple of science fiction for at least a couple of decades, Microsoft's "Bob" was a preliminary (and somewhat rudimentary) attempt to bring social interfaces to the public. While Microsoft is no longer enhancing Bob, other products will be available to take its place.

Sun Microsystems also has a major project in interface technology called "Starfire" (of which a demonstration video is also available). One of the distinguishing characteristics of the Starfire effort is its creators' intention to specifically model user interface technology 10 years in the future (from 1994 when it was first developed, see [Tognazzini 1994]). According to Sun's design team (some of whom came from Apple and Xerox), that future will include tabletop-sized displays, sensors that record gestures made in the air, and, of course, excellent voice recognition. In contrast to other efforts that target an unknown future time or timespan, the user interface designers at Sun went to great pains to portray features that have a basis in existing technology that is more likely than not to be economically and technically viable in 10 years. Their vision is well worth studying.

Much research is also directed to the potential of "virtual reality," already a standard feature of many PC games but not yet a player in strategic systems. The ultimate in "putting the user in the driver's seat," VR approaches can be seen in a very futuristic setting in the movies *Lawnmower Man* and *Virtuosity*.[2] An even better depiction of the use of virtual reality can be seen in the spate of TV shows that have grown up in the post Star Wars era. *Earth 2* (which had only a one-season run!) shows characters using VR in their everyday activities. Marooned on a distant planet that looks suspiciously like Colorado, each wears a communications headset (one ear and one eye piece) that puts them into virtual co-location with each other wherever they are—even

---

2. Readers should note that this is not intended to be an endorsement for viewing movies with a heavy emphasis on gratuitous violence.

on the other side of the galaxy. If you get to see a rerun of the episode containing a gala formal wedding held in VR, you'll understand where this technology is going—and quite possibly within 10 years.[3]

One of the first (if not *the* first) commercial product to use a VR interface to good purpose is Computer Associates's new generation of CA-Unicenter (cleverly called CA-Unicenter/TNG—The Next Generation). This network management product shows a three-dimensional representation of your network configuration with machines and connections in a perspective view. Network managers can move through space, stopping at a server or a router to check its status and operational parameters. A similar approach is starting to show up in data analysis software, where the user can literally "zoom in" on each dimension of the data. While this may be pushing the metaphor, this type of interface is certainly easy to use and often much more intuitive than other approaches to analyzing complex multi-dimensional databases. What all this means for the development of future business systems, however, is still an open question.

All these efforts in advanced user interface technology show that the graphical user interface was only the first step in making the computer easier to understand and use. The search is on for the "perfect user interface," the one where the impedance between human and computer is lowered to zero and the full value of the computer system can be used effectively. Some researchers believe that is when we will stop talking about problems with computer-user interfaces because the computer will have disappeared from view and become an integral part of every device we use. When that happens, we will only talk about *user interfaces*.

---

3. In case you don't get to see this sequence, here is a brief description: the scene opens on the happy couple cutting the cake. The band strikes up a waltz, and the couple, in full wedding attire, joins in, along with all the celebrants in various types of formal wear. The scene fades out and then back in on a slightly different scene as you realize that you had been viewing their virtual reality and that everyone is just where you expect them to be, marooned on the planet Colorado, wearing their VR headsets, moving to imaginary music from an imaginary band and wearing imaginary formals. Some people even have imaginary partners. It is an incredibly convincing portrayal of group virtual reality as it might someday be.

36 Intelligent Agents

One way of increasing a system's value is to design the system to learn—that is, to become better at its tasks each time it performs them. The idea of the "intelligent agent," software that assists the end-user—and becomes better at it as time goes on—has moved from science fiction to reality.

Intelligent agents (sometimes called "autonomous agents") are supposed to turn the computer from a tool, where all tasks are initiated by the user, into a cooperative partner, where some of the tasks are initiated by agents acting on your behalf. For example, I currently search several databases on a regular basis to look for articles on new information systems technology. Sometimes I have my assistant (a human being) do this for me. With appropriate software, I can now have my computer agent search those same databases, using criteria approximating my own, and let me know when it has found articles that would be interesting to me. If its programming is sufficiently advanced, the agent will learn to modify its search criteria when I reject certain articles or ask for more. It can even be programmed to search for additional databases that should be of interest. This software is not only immediately valuable, but its value increases with time as it learns to do its job better. Several companies are already selling software that approximates these functions.

Intelligent agents are still in their infancy, and many problems remain to be solved. A recent issue of the *Communications of the ACM* highlighted this technology, and an article by Pattie Maes pinpointed the main areas for research:

> *…Two main problems have to be solved when building software agents. The first problem is that of competence: how does an agent acquire the knowledge it needs to decide when to help the user, what to help the user with and how to help the user? The second problem is that of trust: how can we guarantee the user feels comfortable delegating tasks to an agent? [Maes 1994]*

Software agents won't soon replace human agents, but they will start to handle some of their tasks. This is certainly a user interface technology that has the potential to create value.

Managing the New Information Systems Technology

Successful implementation of new information systems technology is dependent not only on understanding the macro issues but also on dealing with specific project management issues. This section discusses several that keep coming up again and again in projects involving the new information systems technology:

- What is the cost of deploying new information systems technology?
- How should you measure new information systems technology?
- How do you deal with the risks in using new information systems technology?
- How should you organize to use the new information systems technology most effectively?

Dealing with these issues does not require formulating an entirely new approach to project management, but rather the application of existing principles in new ways. And that is what this section is intended to help you do.

Now I'll manage better this time, Alice said to herself, and began by taking the little golden key...

Alice's Adventures in Wonderland

37 The True Cost of New Technology

In the past several years, the trade press and various industry analysts have reported varying results when analyzing the costs of implementing systems using client/server, object technology, and other components of the new information systems technology. They range from showing savings (over existing technology) of 50 percent to 75 percent to additional costs of up to 70 percent (as in a recent Gartner Group study [Dec 1995]). The debate, therefore, continues over whether you save money in using new information systems technology or not. And, depending on how and what you count, the answer could be either one.

There are several essential factors to consider when entering this debate.

- Are you interested in costs attributed to the IS department or total cost to the organization?
- Are you concentrating on costs attributed to a particular project or to the entire IS organization?
- Are you looking at development costs or life-cycle costs?
- Are you including costs of overlapping operation of systems to be replaced, or only of the new system?
- And, are you concerned about costs only, or are you balancing them against benefits?

These will seem to be somewhat basic questions (they are), but I have seen cost analyses used to justify (or condemn) systems without being clear on these points.

If you are interested in how to create value with the new information systems technology, you have to look at all the costs and all the benefits. This doesn't necessarily mean that you will evaluate every project in this way, but it does mean that the organization should understand the structure of the costs and benefits and the timeline. In fact, many new technology projects are not "cost justified" at all—they are conducted to satisfy some other perceived need of the organization or of its executives—but that is a whole other topic.

For example, when you introduce new information systems technology to the IS department, you can count on a significant start-up and training period with associated start-up costs. It is not unusual to take six to nine months of "getting ready" before you can begin developing your first major system (although you may have done some prototypes or even some fairly small operational systems before then). Here's why.

- You must first determine what new information systems technology you are going to use (e.g., is it going to be object-oriented, object-like, or object sort of?).
- You have to evaluate and select vendors for development tools, databases, middleware, and a variety of pieces of software and hardware you never dreamed that you needed.[1]
- You have to purchase sufficient software and hardware for experimentation, training, and, eventually, development (and pay the cost of setting up appropriate purchase arrangements).
- You have to create appropriate infrastructure to keep the hardware and software in operation (LAN operational procedures managed by LAN administrators, "software gurus," etc.).
- You have to train your staff not just in new software development tools but in new approaches to system

---

1. I was recently asked to sign a requisition for a Pentium-based PC with a 64 Mb memory (yes, 64 megabytes) to act as a "systems management" server for our LAN. I wonder how many client/server development plans include systems management servers, let alone ones with 64 Mb (which I am assured is absolutely necessary based on extensive tests of the software with machines in our lab)?

development (something you can't do a week before the project is about to begin).

- You have to develop (or otherwise procure) new methodologies for system development, testing, maintenance (don't forget maintenance!), and system operations.
- You may even have to adapt your new development tools to the peculiarities of your organization (such as naming conventions, file storage locations, etc.)—taking the time of your programmers away from developing the system itself.

In short, beginning to use new information systems technology is a major project unto itself—and that costs.

Once you have passed the start-up period, don't think that your costs will be confined to the development of specific systems. PC and LAN administration has become a major cost in organizations (in some cases, unfortunately, one that is mostly hidden).[2] And this doesn't mean just dealing with the wiring and the central servers: someone has to keep all that software upgraded, those PCs connected, that e-mail flowing, and perform those hundreds of other tasks that make for smooth operations in today's modern organization. The Gartner Group and others have estimated these costs as high as $8000 per user per year!

Even then you aren't necessarily ready to go full bore on implementing a strategic information system. If you are planning on taking advantage of software that you have purchased or previously developed (i.e., "reusing" components), you have to decide how you are going to populate your "reuse library" and how you are going to make it accessible to your staff. If you are purchasing some components (which you most assuredly will), you have to decide which vendors you will use and how you will work with them.[3] If you are developing some components to sat-

---

2. And not just in organizations: how many of you are also serving in the role of home LAN administrators? Believe me, there is a significant (hidden) cost to that as well. [If you can get your hands on the October 1, 1995 *New York Times Business Section,* you might enjoy my column on that topic.]

3. Working closely with vendors is an important determinant of client/server success (as the opposite is often correlated with client/server failure). See Chapter 24 *The Component Approach Creates an IS Technology Supply Chain* on page 160

isfy particular needs for functionality common to your domain, you have to establish the development (and maintenance!) projects to do that. Taking advantage of the component approach to development first requires a significant infrastructure investment. Even if the majority of your reusable components are purchased, you have to work to take advantage of the technology supply chain rather than having it take advantage of you.

Now that your new technology infrastructure is accounted for, you can begin to estimate project development costs. Unfortunately, there aren't many procedures for developing cost estimates for new technology projects (there just aren't that many new technology projects to base them on), so you have to resort to time-tested rules of thumb (although hopefully with somewhat more basis than Dilbert's boss). This is complicated by the need to estimate how much time will be spent in iteration cycles and how much time will be spent in testing and producing successive increments.

DILBERT ©1996. United Features Syndicate.   Reprinted by Permission.

You will have many additional questions to answer about the scope of your estimate:

- Is training the project team in technology specific to the system part of the "project" or part of IS overhead?
- Is creating the project's development environment included? [Even if a client/server development environment exists, every sizable project has many project-specific components that will need to be added.]

- Is the project cost measured on a "direct cost basis," or are other costs to be allocated to the project and counted in its estimate?
- And so on and so forth…

Some of the answers to these questions may be prescribed by IS department policy, but they all have to be addressed or you won't end up with a complete and comparable answer to the question of what the system is going to cost.

Once you have completed a development estimate for your project, you have to deal with the nasty fact that the development period is only a small part of the system's life-cycle. Some of the most compelling arguments for using new information systems technology (particularly object technology) have to do with reduced maintenance costs. If you don't include the maintenance period in your calculations, you are probably overstating the costs of the system versus its benefits.

So these are the major cost drivers in a system life-cycle employing new technology:

- technology selection and start-up
- creation of development environment (including purchased components)
- creation or purchase of "technology infrastructure" (i.e., templates and frameworks)
- staff training
- system development approach (iterative and incremental)
- maintenance of development environment and infrastructure
- maintenance of system

Once you have dealt with all these factors, you are on the way to determining the true cost of using the new information systems technology. Technology costs, however, must be balanced against a lifetime of offsetting cost savings and other benefits. And ultimately, it is those benefits, quantified or not, that will justify the investment.

38 Measuring the New Information Systems Technology

"The number one factor common to companies scoring high in quality was that they were quantitative and had instituted measurement processes." [Dr. Curtis Reimann, 1989 Chairman of the Board of Overseers, Malcolm Baldrige National Quality Award, reported in Walrad 1993]

"When you can measure what you are speaking about, and express it in numbers, you know something about it; but when you cannot measure it, when you cannot express it in numbers, your knowledge is of a meager and unsatisfactory kind..."[Will Thomson, Lord Kelvin][4]

To take the measure of something is to describe it in a way that allows comparison and review. Saying "that house is big" is interesting, but saying that it has 3500 square feet of space allows us to compare that house with others in a much more direct way. While we can debate forever on the meaning of "big," "bigger," and "biggest" (is Bill Gates's new house the biggest?), saying "my house has 3500 sq. ft. and Bill Gates's has 35,000" gives us the data we need to continue the discussion from a common frame of refer-

---

4. Of course, Lord Kelvin also was reputed to have said that "heavier than air flying machines are impossible" (as president of the Royal Society in 1895), so we can justifiably be a little skeptical of his counsel.

ence.[5] The metric "square feet of enclosed space" highlights the size of the house in a way that allows us to subject it to review and comparison.

Measurement and comparison can be important components of the management process—if they support a business purpose or decision and help lead to improvements in the organization. To be effective management tools, therefore, our measurements must tell us how the thing that we are measuring impacts the organization. In regard to the use of new information systems technology, what kind of impact should we expect? It should:

- make systems easier to use,
- make systems more readily responsive to changing business situations,
- provide new mechanisms for communicating with customers,
- aid the introduction of new products and services, and
- provide new channels for delivering services to customers.

Our task, therefore, is to come up with a series of measurements that focus on these impacts.

38.1   ON FINDING A MEASUREMENT COMMON GROUND

IS practitioners and researchers have long labored to find common measures of the size of the systems we develop, the effectiveness with which we develop them, and even the impact they have on our organizations. We have used "lines of code" and "lines of code produced per man-month" for years as measures of the size of computer programs and programmer productivity, respectively. We have recently incorporated a better understanding of what we are trying to deliver in systems (i.e. functionality rather than lines of code) by using "function points" and "function points per person-month" (also showing a better understanding of who is doing the delivering.) We have attempted to

---

5.   Although it is a little bit of a stretch to say that anything about Bill Gates's house gives us a common frame of reference. I had the opportunity to see it under construction (from a distance), and the builders were using the same type of self-erecting traveling crane that is used on office buildings.

measure the benefits our systems provide using elaborate calculations of tangible and intangible effects. Despite all our attempts, however, we have failed to create standard basic approaches that are widely accepted and actually used in a majority of IS organizations.[6]

For almost a decade, I have been conducting a wide-ranging although somewhat unscientific survey on IS measurement programs. Whenever I speak at client/server, object technology, and system development conferences, I ask my audiences the following questions:

> *"How many of you know in a quantitative way, using whatever measures you choose, the productivity of your IS department and whether it is improving?"*

> *"How many of you know in a quantitative way, using whatever measures you choose, the quality of systems you produce and whether it is improving?"*

The response of more than two dozen audiences—well over 2500 people—has never been more than 4 percent. A more scientific survey shows much the same thing, with Howard Rubin reporting only 1 percent of more than 4000 senior IS managers having quantitative quality data [Rubin 1995-2].[7] I find this to be truly amazing, particularly in a field with at least some origins in the quantitative sciences and with some pretensions to wanting to improve itself by focusing on the needs of its customers.

The arguments (excuses?) against putting too much effort into information system measurements have to do with the absence of standard definitions and with the difficulty of performing the

---

6. We do, however, have a common measure for reporting on when a system will be completed that seems to be in fairly wide use. The five points on this scale are: (1) "Well, we are just starting testing" (2) "Everything works that we have tested" (3) "Two more weeks." (4) "We're putting out a Beta version tomorrow," and (5) "When did you want it?" These measurement points translate roughly into the following "time to completion": (1) unknown (2) two more weeks (3) two more months (4) two more weeks, and (5) unknown. I'm not taking pot shots at hard-working system testers—I'm just reporting on what I told my supervisors earlier in my career, always with complete faith in my ability to complete my tasks on time.

7. He also reports a somewhat puzzling statistic that 15% of 700 CIOs reported that they could quantify the quality of their applications. I wonder if this is a case of the bosses thinking they know something because the next level down hasn't come clean with what is really going on.

measurements themselves. There is no boiling point or freezing point in systems development to anchor our measurement scales (although initiation of design and beginning of production aren't bad proxies). There is no international standard platinum-iridium bar sitting in Paris to serve as a standard "unit" for a line of code or a function point.[8] And when it comes to determining the impact of information systems on the organization, there are far too many confounding factors to sort it all out.

Those are the excuses. If our industry wants to improve its reputation for delivering value to our end-users, we had better be looking for solutions as well. In an article in *American Programmer,* Capers Jones, the widely acknowledged guru of software measurement, notes that his studies of successful and unsuccessful projects show that lack of historical software measurement data is one of the top ten factors associated with project failure [Jones 1995].[9]

Standard definitions are important, but any organization can find useful measures to adopt within its own boundaries. Even if other organizations have their own definitions (meaning that your measurements may not be comparable externally), you can use yours to take a series of measurements and plot a trend. Even if the metrics gurus are telling you to set up sophisticated data collection processes, you can make simple measurements that don't require adding significantly to your bureaucracy just to collect them. You can be using your measurements while everyone else is arguing over definitions. In my opinion, there are few valid reasons not to measure and lots of reasons to do so.

38.2   SIZE IS THE FIRST MEASUREMENT ISSUE

One factor is common to all of the measures and measurement strategies and, therefore, deserves a discussion of its own: "size."

---

8. Yes, I know that that good ol' bar is no longer the international standard for the meter. But how many of you carry around meter sticks measured out to the "1,650,763.73 wavelengths of the orange-red light of the excited krypton atom of mass number 86"?

9. Another one is particularly interesting: naive senior executives. It is not only project management, or even IS management, who have to work at understanding the new information systems technology and what it offers, but senior line-of- business executives as well.

Without being able to discuss the size of information systems, it is hard to come up with appropriate measures to judge their value or anything else. Size is the normalizing factor that allows us to compare one system to another without simply saying that bigger systems in general create more value than smaller systems.

Size, however, is one of the most difficult things to measure about information systems. Rubin's study cited above notes that only 25 percent of senior IS managers have data on the size of their IS asset base. Perhaps the difficulty of measuring size is a dissuading factor, but that doesn't diminish the importance of knowing how big your systems are.

The size of a system is definitely in the eyes of the beholder— and those eyes are often in quite different places. Here are some of the quantitative answers I have received in response to the question "how big is this system?" [10]

- "We counted 12,822 function points."
- "There are 256 thousand lines of source code."
- "The development project took twelve months."
- "The project cost $3 million."
- "The development team has 15 people on it."
- "There are over 450 windows and 120 reports."
- "There are 247 programs and 42 databases."
- "It runs on an XYZ 9500 with 64 Mb of memory connected to an ABC database server with 2 gigs of storage."
- "The code library is over two megabytes."
- "The compiled code modules are 800K."
- "The design document is 550 pages."
- "It took us two days just to load the data into the production database."

---

10. In trying to get a handle on the size issue, I will often ask somewhat open-ended questions (at first) to see what the developer thinks about. If the answer isn't sufficiently detailed or doesn't address the real question I thought I was asking, I can always ask another, more specific question. In the meantime, I have learned something about this developer's point of view. At one time or another, I have been given all the answers listed. I always asked at least one more question.

I view each of these answers as providing a valid measure of the size of the system, albeit an incomplete one. In this, I am taking exception to the "function point" lobby, which tries to compute a single composite measure of system size (and complexity), good for all purposes.[11] Function points are a useful and important measure, in my opinion, but not the only useful and important measure. My claim is that information is contained in each of the answers just presented—certainly a lot more than in "the system is really big," another answer I have received on occasion.[12]

Have you ever noticed that nothing really big or complex is described with only a single size measure: cruise boats advertise their length, weight, number of passengers, and number of crew; the interior of an airplane is described by its number of seats, configuration, and height;[13] office buildings note their total area but also their number of floors; and if a man wants a properly fitting shirt, he had better buy one classified by at least a neck size and a sleeve length rather than by a single composite measure.

Why should we presume to subsume all the complexities of a computer system into a single size measure? It would be nice and certainly would be simple. But it would also obscure a lot of very valuable information about the system, not to mention creating a fair amount of controversy about the ways in which such a single

---

11. The function point measure was created by Allan Albrecht of IBM in 1979 and has since achieved a good measure of acceptance, even spawning the International Function Point Users Group (in which I sponsor our company's membership—I think their work is mostly very helpful to the industry). Function points measure the output of the IS department by counting the "functions" delivered to users. In this sense, function points measure the size and complexity of information systems. Number of input transactions, reports, queries, and files are summed to arrive at a "function count" that is then adjusted by 14 factors (including transaction rate, installation ease, and performance) to account for system complexity. For detailed information on counting function points, see http://www.bannister.com/ifpug/home/docs/docs.html. For more of my views on the use of function points, see *Measuring IS Development* on page 243.

12. See *An Aside About "Big" Systems* on page 238.

13. Even freighters are described by more than their volume, since the number and types of containers that they are outfitted to carry is an important characteristic of their size.

measure would best be computed.[14] Although the respondents to my size question were all giving me valid size measures, they also were giving me an incorrect answer by giving me only one: without knowing my particular reason for asking, they could not have known that their answers were sufficient for my purposes (although, presumably, they were sufficient for their own).

Let's look at some of these system "sizes." If you are concerned about how easy it will be to recreate the database if it should fail, then the answer about how long it takes to load is an important size measure. If you are trying to gauge this system against others you are familiar with, then any of the measures about function points, lines of code, development time, etc., might suffice—as long as they provide comparable measures to the ones you know about for other systems. Clearly, none of the answers by itself provides a complete picture of the size of the system. We have to provide further information about why we are taking this measure of the system to know that we are providing sufficient measurements. Measurements are not ends unto themselves, but rather means to accomplish some task or process improvement.

Fundamentally, size is a normalizing factor. We need to know some measure of size to compute unit values of productivity (e.g., dollars spent per function point developed), operational efficiency (e.g., compute seconds per transaction), and value to the organization (e.g., dollars of benefits per dollar invested). Note that each of these examples used a different normalizing measure, that is, a different measure of size. We also need to know a system's size to compare it to other systems. My view is that we need to have several measures of size available to serve the different purposes that we may have in measuring and managing systems—and we hamper our ability to achieve those purposes without a good variety of them.

---

14. This is, of course, the same premise applied by Kaplan and Norton in suggesting the balanced scorecard approach to organizational measurement: trying to boil everything down to a single profitability measure (as some managers try to do) is often counterproductive.

38.2.1   An Aside About "Big" Systems

I am constantly amazed at the number of times I have heard that "the system we are developing is really big." This is most often stated in a very authoritarian tone as a way of justifying some strategy, decision, or delay; and it is intended by the speaker to be an adequate and complete statement in its own right. My experience is that most such statements have little or no quantitative data to back them up, and do not provide justification for whatever it is that the speaker has in mind. Size and complexity (because complexity is often what is really being talked about), as well as many other characteristics of systems, *can* be quantified. Unfortunately, they are often discussed without reference to any specific numbers, and this can lead to major misunderstandings.

...Which reminds me of one of my first job interviews (1968) when the interviewer went on for some time about this "really big system" he wanted me to work on. I was excited about the opportunity because I had just completed my Master's thesis developing a really big system that filled the entire 8K memory of our quite-new Digital Equipment Corporation PDP-8 (it was physically big too, taking up most of a standard-size office). As the interviewer continued to wax eloquent about the implications of his project, I soon realized that I was completely lost.

I asked for clarification:

"Can you tell how big *is* really big *to you; can you give me some numbers?"*

I didn't really care what numbers I was given, just so that I had something to use to anchor my understanding. With the interviewer's answer, I discovered the source of my confusion: his idea of *really big* was a GE-635 mainframe with nine processors (one of the earlier parallel processor systems), each with a 512K word (2Mb) memory, and arranged in a spherical physical configuration via a three-floor computer center (five processors on the middle floor; two each above and below) occupying about half a football field. Processors were big in those days, and the three-floor configuration allowed them to minimize inter-processor wiring distances so that the machine could communicate with itself! My PDP-8 was the puniest of the puny by comparison.

238

A little quantification had gone a long way in reminding me that *big* is in the eye of the beholder—a lesson I have tried to remember and pass on.

38.3   A BALANCED SCORECARD APPROACH TO MEASUREMENT

If you accept the premise that measurement is a necessity, the next question is what to measure. It depends, of course, on what you want to analyze. Managing the appropriate use of new information systems technology means that you should be able to demonstrate how it creates value, presumably more value than older technology—and that means you must measure the value of the systems in which that technology is used.

Measuring value from several points of view and in several ways will help us to understand how and where new information systems technology is most effective. It will also help in making sure that improvements in one measure of value aren't coupled with degradation in another.

- to gauge the value created by improving productivity of the system's end-users, *measure* increased output by those end-users;
- *while* measuring value created by reducing costs (per investment dollar—or pound or mark or escudo);
- *but also* check for value created by increasing revenues (measured by increased revenue per employee, per month, etc.).

Each of these measurements involves money, but we can also use non-monetary measures in determining value.

A simple framework for organizing a multiple measurement approach is the "balanced scorecard" described by Kaplan and Norton [Kaplan 1992]. These authors are studying organizational performance, and they recommend selecting a group of measures to view the organization from four perspectives: *customer*, *internal*, *innovation and learning*, and *financial*. They compare this multi-dimensional approach to viewing instruments in an airplane cockpit. Pilots need information about multiple aspects of their airplane and flight; managers, too need information about multiple aspects of their organizations and performance.

Kaplan and Norton call the results of taking these measures a "balanced scorecard" of the organization's performance.

We can adopt the balanced scorecard approach and adapt it for measuring information systems value.[15] First, we have to determine what perspectives are appropriate for analyzing the system (and the IS function). Then we have to define the measures to be used.

Given our focus on measuring the value that systems bring to the organization, the appropriate perspectives are from:

- *End-users* (the IS customer's view): What do they think about how well systems and the IS organization are fulfilling their functions?
- *Development process* (the internal view): How effectively is IS creating and maintaining systems?
- *Organizational goals*: Are those systems helping the organization to accomplish its goals and increase its value?
- *Financial*: What do systems cost, and is their value significantly greater than their cost?

The measures used in a balanced scorecard for information systems are basically productivity and quality measures. Productivity measures are calculations of outputs divided by inputs. Quality measures are based on the definition of high-quality systems as operating reliably, supporting people in fulfilling their responsibilities efficiently and effectively, and, in general, contributing to the functioning of the organization. Different measures will be required to capture all four viewpoints, and several are possible for each. Figure 65 shows measures that might occur in an IS balanced scorecard (the "customer" referred to in this chart is the organization's customer, not the IS "customer" or end-user).

---

15. Several of my colleagues at AMS have been using the balanced scorecard as they help organizations in "achieving breakthrough performance," a practice area introduced by Fred Forman. Martin Lockett has used this technique extensively with major clients and brought it to AMS. Milt Hess is trying to create balanced scorecards for managing system implementation projects.

Figure 65: Balanced scorecard measures for IS

Viewpoint	Example Measures
End-user	Output (e.g. widgets) per labor dollar input in functional department; end-user satisfaction; and end-user errors and re-work; end-user training required; etc.
IS development process	Output[a] per dollar spent in the IS department; system reliability; problem reports; post-implementation rework; requested changes; etc.
Organizational goals	Customer satisfaction; ability to meet customer demands for new services; change in number of customers; etc.
Financial	Functional department operational costs; revenues per dollar invested in IS; profitability (percent margin); etc.

a. Of course, we have to define "output" from the development process—just what is it that the IS department is creating? Is it systems, lines of code, "function points," or whatever? See the following sections for further discussion.

When all these measures have been collected, the challenge still remains of presenting the results in a way that is both meaningful and easy to understand. Howard Rubin, who discusses many different measures that can be taken about information systems, provides an effective way of presenting the current value of multiple measures. He presents a literal "measurement dashboard," with each measure represented by an instrument face (as on an instrument panel in an automobile or airplane) and each value represented by the placement of the indicator for that instrument (see various issues of his newsletter, *IT Metrics Strategies*, for numerous examples, as well as [Rubin 1995-2]). While the dashboard is a good presentation of one "measurement point" (e.g., this week or this month), it needs to be coupled with graphics that show how the measurements are changing over time. Figure 66 presents part of an IS balanced scorecard using these techniques.

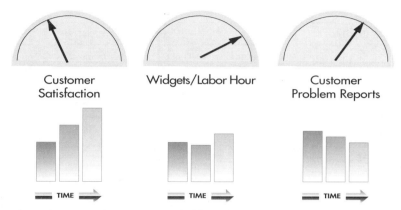

Figure 66: Balanced scorecard presentation dashboard

38.3.2   Measuring the End-User's View

From the end-user point of view, the value of a system is identified with its helping them do their jobs more efficiently and effectively. If the system is targeted to a particular business purpose, such as customer service, then measures will already be in place (e.g., customers served per employee) that can be used to give a "before" and "after" view of departmental productivity and quality. If the system is more widely used, such as a publicly available system for ordering from a catalog, then you can take direct user surveys to determine how the system is performing. Do the users feel that they are spending less time on filling out their orders? You could ask them to rate the improvement (or lack thereof) on a simple scale to form a measure of this attribute. Although objective measures of value from the end-user view are desirable, subjective user surveys are often more practical.

End-user survey techniques have been widely discussed and used in regard to information systems.[16] Most surveys ask questions about the value of specific system features as well as general question about how well the system supports end-user activities, how easy it is to learn and understand, how reliably it

---

16. For an example of a user satisfaction survey and a discussion of its use, see the March, 1995, issue of *IT Metrics Strategies*.

operates, etc. A questionnaire before and after a new system or major enhancement has been in operation for several months will provide the most direct data about that system. You can also take annual surveys to collect trend information about the overall performance of the IS department.

38.3.3   Measuring IS Development

The typical IS department has lagged other parts of the organization in establishing and measuring productivity and quality. In fact, one of the biggest obstacles is simply defining what is meant by productivity and quality in the context of systems development and system support.

"Output" is the numerator of any productivity measure, whether it be revenue per employee or widgets produced per hour. Early attempts at establishing productivity measures for IS focused on technical output, such things as lines of code, programs, windows, and reports.[17] More recently, IS organizations have been focusing on customer-centric measures of their output, that is, how much functionality has been delivered to the end-users. Here, the discussion focuses on functionality of the systems rather than sheer size in any technical sense. The problem is finding a measure that can be calculated for many different types of systems that will present a reliable index of their functionality.

The *function points* measure has been presented as representing a reasonable proxy for total system functionality. While function points is being promoted as a standard measure, and can be very useful, it still runs into difficulty in trying to merge so many factors into a single measure. For example, a student information system for a university had half the number of function points of a billing system for a telephone company. By other measures, such as lines of code (they are both written in

---

17. Even here, definition is difficult. Just how many lines of code does your system have? Do you count comments, data definitions, multiple statements on one line, multiple lines for one statement? In my view, it doesn't really matter, as long as you tell me how you counted and you also give me some of the intermediate data (separate counts for each) so that I can draw my own conclusions. The problem is that most people are driven to citing a single number.

the same language), the billing system was 500 percent larger than the student system. The billing system also cost 10 times the student system, took a proportionally greater effort to develop, and probably serves 50 times as many end-users. My point is that no one of these measures (function points, lines of code, cost, number of users) is sufficient to tell us how to compare the output of the IS department in delivering these two systems. I prefer to use function points as one among several measures of output, along with an intelligent analysis of the meaning and applicability of each.

Unfortunately, we encounter similar problems when trying to define measures of system quality. All of the "ilities" could come into play: usability, flexibility, portability, reliability, maintainability, etc. All contribute in some way to quality, and many can be measured quantitatively.[18] Problem reports and change requests, for example, can be used to collect statistics on reliability and maintainability, answering questions such as:

- Are systems installed today experiencing fewer start-up problems than systems installed a year ago?
- Do change requests indicate user dissatisfaction with current system features (indicating a low-quality system) or expanded ideas about how successful system features can be improved (indicating a high-quality system)?

Each answer contributes to our understanding of system quality and how it is changing over time.

38.3.4   Organizational Goal Measurements

From the organizational point of view, systems have to provide value by furthering the organization's general and specific goals. Of course, this is easiest to measure in organizations that have specific quantifiable goals, but can also be shown in a qualitative way even if they don't.

Understanding the value of a system in accomplishing an organization's goals means comparing how much information

---

18. Although, I wouldn't know how to begin to combine them into a single quality measure, nor do I think we should even try (same point as above).

systems *could* have contributed to any particular goal to how much the system in question actually did contribute.[19] This approach gets at the questions of absolute contribution (is this an area where a good system could be highly valuable?) and actual contribution (what did this system do?). Simple quantitative scales for answering these questions will allow you to come up with a value score for a particular system as well as a comparison measure from one system area to another.

Even though some systems contribute to organizational goals only indirectly (for example, the payroll system), others are specifically oriented to better meeting customer demands for products and services (customer service systems, order entry systems, customer information systems, and the newest systems that provide direct access to customers via the Internet and the World Wide Web). Both types of systems have an impact, but one is easier to measure than the other.

38.3.5   Financial Measurements

Whether your organization uses formal return-on-investment calculations or not, your balanced scorecard should still contain information on the cost and revenue impact of your system. Some systems will result in lower operational costs for the department they service, whereas others may be direct revenue generators. It never hurts to be able to expound on the direct dollar impact when discussing new systems.

It has been fairly standard practice to attempt to estimate the organizational costs that a yet-to-be-developed system will save, or perhaps the additional costs that it will help the organization avoid. Cost savings are stated in dollar terms and are typically based on reduced personnel, inventory, accounts receivable, waste material, or the like. In some organizations, it is even standard practice to measure those savings after the system is in production for some period of time. Both practices are recom-

---

19. The Gartner Group reports on one firm's efforts to assess the value provided by the entire IS department in this way via very specific questioning of key employees in different parts of the business and then calculating a single composite measure of IS effectiveness (see [Rosser 1993]). While I am clearly opposed to this type of "shmushing" together of different measurements, I do think they had a good basic approach.

mended, and standard management analysis techniques are generally applicable.

A more difficult measurement, but one much more appealing in today's competitive environment, is the calculation of additional revenue that a new system will bring to the organization. For example, a Web-based ordering system for a securities firm is expected to bring in new customers and result in additional orders of higher volume from existing customers. While this can be estimated using whatever growth factors seem reasonable, measuring it will require both a baseline and sorting out all other possible factors that might have led to any increases (such as increased advertising or improved customer service procedures). The point is that modern systems are more and more becoming part of the "products and services" that an organization provides and providing direct revenue benefit.

Even though all measures of value can be reduced to financial terms (after all, improved productivity and quality have monetary value), this part of the balanced scorecard is the place to present those factors that are most usually expressed in monetary terms. They provide one more piece of the puzzle of how a system creates value.

38.4   DOES IT REALLY MATTER? CONTRARY VIEWS

Does all this measurement really matter? Some say that information systems technology appears to have no effect on the organization, so why bother? I have a hard time reconciling that view with what I see going on in organizations around me, but it is worth a short digression to air the opposing viewpoints.

Paul Strassman, one of the industry's more visible former CIOs, has studied the relationship among revenues, profits, and IT spending in more than 50 industrial sectors. His data show that profitability is

> *"totally unrelated to the amount of information technology [a sector] employs. The only plausible explanation for any differences [in profitability] is the manner in which any enterprise has taken a unique approach to combining its various elements of people, skill, motivation, and technology to deliver a*

result that differs from what competitors do with the identical resources." [Strassman 1995]

Prof. Eric Brynjolfsson of MIT's Sloan School of Management has done statistical analyses on more detailed data and came to somewhat opposite conclusions [Brynjolfsson 1993]. In particular, Brynjolfsson and his associates looked at firm-level data rather than sector-level data and found that computer technology adds significantly to output—perhaps even more than spending on other types of capital investment. One hypothesis these researchers suggest is that firms spending more on IS may take customers from firms that spend less, without significantly expanding output in the sector as a whole. So while computer spending may not appear to improve productivity in a particular sector when compared with others, it does improve productivity in a firm when measured versus others.

And, of course, that is the point.

39 The Problem with Pilot Projects Is Picking the Wrong One

Standard advice to organizations beginning with a new information systems technology is to try it on a pilot project. The pilot project is an important step in evaluating the technology as well as in learning how it helps to create business value. Unfortunately, many organizations take that advice and then proceed to make a major mistake by selecting the wrong project as the pilot. They either select the wrong business problem, the wrong time, the wrong team, or some combination of all three.

A common mistake is to try to set up a "typical" situation to pilot a new technology. That is, the organization takes the next project in its queue, with whatever manager and team it is planning to assign, and says "go for it." Maybe the project will benefit from using the new technology (i.e., using the new technology will bring additional business value), but maybe it won't. Maybe the project manager will be committed to succeeding with the new technology, but maybe he won't. Maybe the project team will want to be guinea pigs, but most likely they won't! If you are interested in seeing the new technology at its best, you need to handpick the project, the manager, the team, and the timing. Once you have established what it can do, you can work backwards to determine if this technology will have a similar impact when unleashed on the rest of your organization.

Select pilot projects that are performing work which will benefit from the specific tools you are looking at. A project team that is under the gun with a tight deadline or a difficult end-user will likely view the introduction of new methods or tools as a burden they don't need. A good way to turn a project manager off to the entire idea of new technology is to force the use of new tools and techniques onto an already difficult situation.

Find a team that thinks this technology will help them, and the process will become much more than a lab-type exercise. A team performing a business process reengineering (BPR) study for the production department of a manufacturing company may see a way to save significant time and effort by learning and using a new BPR tool. They can then feed their impressions back to those individuals who are charged with looking for the "ideal" product—and perhaps improve the one under study if that is eventually chosen to be rolled out to the rest of the IS organization.

This scenario also illustrates another key factor in doing a successful evaluation of new information systems technology. Make sure the pilot project is staffed by "can do" people who are well versed in your development techniques—you don't want your evaluators still figuring out why they need an object model if they are supposed to be evaluating how well a particular tool provides object-modeling capabilities.

Goldberg and Rubin provide excellent advice on picking pilot projects. They focus on object technology projects, but their prescription carries over to any new technology pilot [Goldberg and Rubin 1995, p.72–73].

- Avoid trivial projects, or projects perceived to be trivial.
- Avoid overly critical projects.
- Don't replace the most optimized legacy system.
- Choose a project with sufficient visibility to ensure desired resources and influence.
- Choose a problem that [the particular technology] is good at handling.
- Choose a project that will last long enough to build team skills.
- Accomplish something tangible early and often.

- Make sure that the project schedule fits with the organization's needs.
- Don't expect to obtain reusable [assets].

This list of do's and don'ts is really just to remind you that a pilot project is an important step in the analysis and introduction of new technology, but not the only step. Follow these rules and you will quickly find the pilot project that will show you whether your new technology is a winner.

40 Risk: Since You Can't Avoid It, Manage It

No systems development project is risk-free. Projects employing new information systems technologies are riskier than average. Given the number and types of components that go into a client/server system, you are likely to be breaking new ground (i.e., using some combination of hardware and software components that no one has ever tried to use together before) in every project you do for the next several years.[20] And based on the rate of introduction of new componentry, you are likely to be breaking new ground with every project you participate in for the remainder of your career!

So what is the proper approach to dealing with the risk of using the new information systems technology? Simple: since you can't avoid it, manage it. Too many projects pay lip service to understanding the risks they are taking on, only to find themselves in a great deal of pain when one of those alligators crawls out of the swamp and bites them in the rump. "An ounce of prevention is worth a pound of cure" was never spoken in a more meaningful setting than in a client/server implementation.

---

20. One of my jobs at AMS involves participating in architecture and development strategy reviews of major projects. There was a time when I would come out of such meetings and send the project manager a note listing all the "ground breakers" he or she was taking on. On one such project, I noted 17 (a record at that time). The project manager distributed copies to everyone on the team and used it as a checklist during development to make sure that the team had a plan for dealing with (or eliminating) each one. The project was ultimately very successful and to this day remains a model of appropriate use and management of new information systems technology.

What does it mean to manage risk? Basically, it calls for having an explicit process (as discussed in [Hess 1993] and [Statz 1995]):

- to understand what the risks to successful completion are,
- to evaluate what the impact of each might be;
- to analyze how likely each is to happen;
- to review what steps you will take to minimize both the likelihood and severity; and,
- to decide what to do about each potential disaster if it actually happens!

If you are going to understand the risks to successful completion of the system, you first have to understand what is meant by "successful completion." One of the biggest points of contention in post-project reviews is whether the system met the end-users' expectations or not, primarily because it is now determined that the project team did not have a perfect view of what those expectations were in the first place. *"Oh, is that what you meant?" "But I thought you understood that we had to have it work like the old systems." "How come the system isn't available 24 hours a day?"* These are all indications that a definitive statement of success (i.e., meeting end-user expectations) wasn't really agreed upon at the outset.

Assuming you have done this, how do you identify risks to success? Beginning with each of the identified success criteria or end-user expectations, look both for specific events that might occur and for generally known factors (e.g., a project schedule known to be overly ambitious) that might work to prevent your meeting expectations. Events are everything from acts of God (a tornado wipes out your development shop) to sub-level performance (the programming team won't be able to finish coding in the allotted time; the hardware vendor misses delivery dates). These events can also be classified as to the level of control and influence you have over them (presumably you can influence your programmers more than your hardware vendor—and both of them more than God). With a little effort, you and your team will have before them a fairly long list of events and known situations and a statement of the risks they might engender:

Expectation: The order entry system will be operational for the Christmas shopping season.

Event: The hardware supplier doesn't make delivery of all required equipment on the agreed schedule.

Situation: Temporary customer service personnel have been hired with little time to train them in the new system.

Risk: We may not have not enough workstations and customer service personnel available to handle expected holiday orders.

The next steps in the risk analysis are to determine possible consequences, severity, and risk mitigation strategies for each risk.

Consequences: Lost orders will result in lost current revenues and possibly lost future revenue if customers go to competitors.

Probability of occurrence: (1) Hardware manufacturer has always been on time before—unlikely. (2) Time to train customer service personnel is limited—likely.

Severity: Very serious.

Mitigation strategies: (1) Talk with hardware manufacturer to emphasize importance of this delivery schedule; get contractual assurances. (2) Train more trainers; develop simplified curriculum for new system; train existing personnel sooner so they can help new people.

Based on your list of risks, you can formulate your risk management plan. You can develop risk mitigation strategies that:

- reduce the likelihood of identified events,
- reduce the impact of known situations,
- reduce uncertainly (perhaps by spending money to buy more information),[21]

---

21. Just as farmers do in buying commercial weather forecasts rather than relying on those they get for free. Presumably they think that they can reduce uncertainty this way, and that is certainly an appropriate risk mitigation strategy for a risky business.

- generate new options (which have different risk characteristics), or
- just change expectations, that is, make sure expectations are aligned with reality!

All of these are legitimate since all reduce uncertainty and negative consequences.

Managing risk is not a one-time event to be performed at a single point in the development cycle. You have to reevaluate your risks and risk mitigation strategies regularly. Particularly in the realm of the new information systems technologies, events happen, situations change, and the impact of various factors on the success of your project is constantly changing. Successful risk management is a process and requires eternal vigilance.

It's 11 o'clock. Do you know where your project's risk manager is?

41 The New IS Organization

The new information systems technology is creating a new IS organization. Or perhaps more accurately, our search for how best to use the new technology effectively is leading us to redefine the titles, roles, and hierarchy that have grown up over the past 25 years. The requirements of existing positions are changing, and an equal number of new positions will be required.

There are two key ways in which the IS organization is being affected as the new technologies discussed in this book are introduced:

- The basic concept of the project team, now widely (but alas not universally) accepted, is being redefined.
- The generalist position of programmer and analyst is changing and sometimes being replaced with a variety of specialist positions.

It is no longer sufficient for a project team to be created from scratch to work fairly independently on the design and implementation of a new system. The IS focus on reuse and components means that this team must be much more integrated into the general structure of the IS strategy and that teams working on individual systems cannot work independently of each other.

The general concept is not new—we have had the database administration team working in partnership with the project team for many years. What is new is the number of disciplines for which this will now be the case, with the prototyping team, the framework (or component) building team, the user interface design team, the usability testing team, and the reuse team (reuse librarians) all being candidates. The base project team becomes the business application (component assembly) team as well as the systems integration team.

Each team has many development and management techniques in common but also many that are distinct to their own disciplines.[22] As each specialist team grows in experience, it further establishes its role in the implementation of new systems, with the entire project team taking on more and more of the role of the integrator of all the disciplines.

As those disciplines multiply, the division of staff into programmers, analysts (or programmer-analysts), and technical specialists is similarly changing with the introduction of more specialists. The entire balance of generalists versus specialists is changing as more and more specialized technologies have to be dealt with. New positions and roles are becoming commonplace, including framework programmers, object analysts, and a myriad of new technical specialists (e.g., the Sybase specialist, the Powerbuilder specialist, the TCP/IP specialist). Add to this list system architects, object librarians, GUI designers, object designers, object developers (builders), component assemblers, object czars (every object project needs one to be successful), network support specialists, risk managers, and dozens of other specialties with their own specialists—and you will find that everyone in the organization has a different title than everyone else!

At the same time as manufacturing organizations are reducing their hyper-specialization and division of labor, IS organizations seem be experiencing a significant increase in the division of labor. Whether this will ultimately turn out to be counter-productive (as happened in the automobile industry) remains to be seen. In the meantime, managing staff resources will become more difficult as we try to fill each different role, often with little or no backup. Our industry is in a state of flux as to personnel and organizational structure. It is one of the key areas requiring management attention as we introduce new information systems technology.

---

22. There was a time when football players performed both offensive and defensive tasks. The separation of teams into two squads came about when it was recognized that not only did each player need different skills, but different coaching and management were also required.

42 Legal Issues in the World of Components

Why a section on legal issues in a book on information systems technology? Because the new component construction approaches mean that long-standing approaches to writing software license agreements will have to change dramatically. And organizations that are not aware of what they are dealing with are walking into a potential mine field.

Legal issues are everywhere. A single issue of *Computerworld* carried these items.

- Copying news articles from the Internet or an on-line service and distributing them to your colleagues is illegal. Three different organizations (Knight-Ridder, the Copyright Clearinghouse Center, and the Intellectual Property Licensing Agency) are working on "pay per view" schemes. ("On-line pay per view: Helping IS stay above the copyright law," p. 58)

- The Pentagon is seeking legal advice on the definition of war as it applies to "information warfare." If someone "invades" the Federal Reserve System and causes electronic and economic havoc, what should or can the armed forces do about it? ("New laws sought for info warfare," p. 55)

- Software to control network user access to license-controlled software is being upgraded to include chargeback capability as well as license metering. This could open the way to usage-based pricing as well as to number-of-simultaneous users pricing. ("Horizons unleashes metering with a twist," p. 49)

257

- A company producing virus detection software is threatened with lawsuits over claims it is making about the efficacy of its product. ("InVircible: Invincible or irresponsible?" p. 41)
- In addition to the usual reports of buyouts and mergers, this one adds a little twist: Microsoft purchased $90 million of convertible preferred stock of Wang Laboratories, thereby acquiring a 10 percent ownership stake. This purchase was in settlement of a patent infringement suit brought by Wang against Microsoft. ("Wang stake sold," p. 32)
- Release 1.2 of the Open Software Foundation's Distributed Computing Environment software was delayed by at least six months due to development contract disputes between IBM (the project leader) and other developers. ("DCE software delays disappoint users," p. 10)
- Widespread use of the Internet is making a mockery of state and even national differences in laws related to access to information. Material and activities (such as on-line gambling) deemed legal in one jurisdiction may be quite illegal in another, much to the consternation of law-enforcement authorities and the occasional detriment of the Internet surfer. Court cases are just the beginning as we move to significant changes in laws and international treaties. ("Internet tramples legal jurisdictions," p. 1)
- The Prodigy on-line service lost a $200 million libel suit (still being appealed) when the court ruled that its efforts to edit on-line content of posted messages makes it a publisher subject to current libel laws. Corporate and other organizations building databases on the Internet are particularly concerned about the implications of this ruling for them. Will they be liable if a Web site referenced on their Web pages contains libelous material? ("Prodigy ruling could chill IS plans," p. 1)
- Dun & Bradstreet is suing a small consulting company over potentially illegal modifications it made to D&B software and passed on to end-users. More interesting is that several of those end-users are being asked to supply documents and code related to the suit, at no small cost in time and

effort to those end-users. ("D&B software customers dragged into code lawsuit," p. 24)

- LAN Administrators working with the latest versions of Novell's network operating system are concerned about the ease with which security can be breached. In addition, system functions make it easy to accidentally grant improper rights to resources on the network (including files). ("Stealth users pose threat to Novell 4," p.1, and "Utility detects stealth users," p. 131) [*Computerworld*, Vol. 29, No. 23, June 5, 1995]

The range of issues that these articles raise (all from a single issue of a popular trade periodical!) is mindboggling:

- Software licensing
- Copyright
- Patents
- Information access
- Privacy
- Services contracts
- Libel
- Pornography

And a year later, all are still at the top of our consciousness, with one (pornography on the Internet) having achieved national notoriety as the subject both of a Congressionally sponsored law in the United States and a court decision ruling it unconstitutional.

Taken individually, each item raises a concern about doing business with the new information systems technology. Taken together, they paint a bleak picture for the near future. Either we are going to see a significant increase in lawsuits between information providers and users and between software providers and users, or a significant increase in law-making (probably followed by lawsuits challenging the legality of the laws). Either way, our bills for legal advice and counsel are going through the roof.

42.1   WHO OWNS WHAT?

A particularly challenging legal issue in the age of objects, component construction, and reuse is sorting out who owns what components of a system, or the components of the components, etc.

Take the following situation (depicted in Figure 67). Company A develops an object class library that it licenses to Company B. Company B modifies the classes (both by inheritance and extension) and incorporates these classes into an application product that it sells to Company C. Company C incorporates the application into a system that it uses to process its own work and the work of "subscribers" to its processing service. Sound unusual? It is not. Many banks and securities firms are today providing just such systems to handle the accounts of others in their industry. Whether they are legally entitled to do so, or are protected in appropriate ways by their license agreements, is an open question. Make it a little more interesting by saying that Company A got some of its code from a posting on the Internet by an employee of Company D and you've got an even more "real-world" situation.

Most of the software licenses in effect today were written to license software developed entirely by one organization to be used without modification by the organization buying the license. These assumptions are almost the opposite of what we can expect in the world of client/server systems.

One of the basic tenets of object technology and component construction is that software will be "written" by assembling components from many sources and that base objects will be modified to suit the needs of the developers. This development approach requires different licensing clauses that are only now making their way into standard agreements. A few examples should suffice to raise the visibility of the issues involved.

Take warranties. In a legacy environment, it was typical for a software vendor to guarantee that software would work according to the manuals on the hardware specified in the license agreement. In the world of client/server, with its thousands of potential hardware environments, it is highly unusual for a software vendor to warrant that their software will work at all, let alone on the hardware that you might purchase next year.

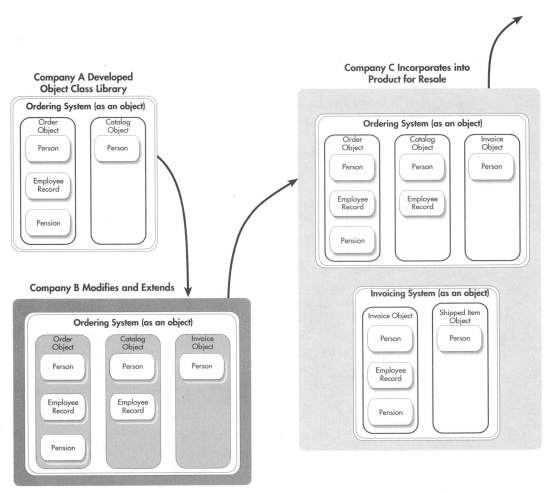

Figure 67: Who owns what?

In the legacy world, one usually had a maintenance clause (which you paid extra for) that said the software vendor would upgrade their system to work with the supported versions of operating system and database management system supplied by the appropriate vendor, such as IBM. Since IBM didn't change its operating systems and database management systems very often, and when it did, it still supported the older versions for at least a couple of years, this was a clause that most software vending organizations could live with. Try to get someone to commit today that they will upgrade their software to work with the latest version of all the other software they depend on and you will have a very difficult case. Take, for example, one of the new client/server development tools (PowerBuilder, SQL Windows, etc.) that operates with at least a dozen different database management systems. It may be a year after a new release comes out from one of the DBMS vendors before these tools will have the ability to use all the new DBMS features—or in some cases to run at all. The tool vendor should want to satisfy you, the customer, but the task of keeping up with everything going on in dozens of other software organizations is just too daunting.

One last area for concern is liability. As software becomes strategic to more and more organizations, we are beginning to see more suits brought for copyright infringement, misappropriation of trade secrets, and other liability issues. Once again, when the software being licensed was solely the property of the licensing party (and when that party was a multi-million dollar publicly traded firm), it was relatively easy to negotiate an acceptable clause. Now the issue is whether the licensing party has the ability to "pass through" the liability to the initial developer. In our example above, if a copyright problem is found to exist in the class library supplied by Company A (say, a suit brought by Company D), what can Company C do about it, especially if Company A is a four person firm operating out of someone's garage? Company C may find itself having to buy its way out of a messy situation (shown in Figure 68).

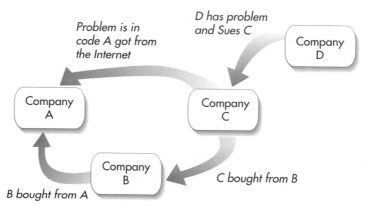

Figure 68: Who has the liability?

I am not saying that all or even any of these difficulties will arise in contracting for software using the new information systems technologies. I am saying that there is more going on than meets the eye and all the legal issues haven't been worked out.

Conclusion: Entering an Era of Constant Change

As organizations recognize the speed at which their businesses are changing, they place higher demands on IS departments to commit to shorter development cycle times and to meet those shortened targets with greater regularity. IS departments, in turn, are searching for the "agile" tools and methods that will allow them to meet those commitments. They want development techniques that can cope with the ever-changing business environment, and tools that are designed to work well with those techniques. They similarly want to work with agile vendors: hardware and software vendors who can respond to their needs, and systems integrators who are adept at synthesizing that hardware and software into workable systems.

> *Tut, tut, child,* said the Duchess. *Everything's got a moral, if only you can find it.* `

Alice's Adventures in Wonderland

Agility implies almost constant change. It is not sufficient to introduce one set of changes and wait for them to have an effect: planning for the next set of changes must already be underway. And when it comes to new information systems technology, the change cycles are measured in increasingly shorter time frames—eventually devolving to almost constant change.

Why is this true? As a direct result of the use of the new information systems technology,

- systems should be easier to use—via *advanced user interfaces*—and that should make it easier to communicate with customers, perhaps directly as over the *World Wide Web*, or indirectly via better identification of customer needs—via *data mining*;

- systems should be more responsive to changing business situations, that is, adaptability should be built in—via the use of *architected client/server* applications that effectively merge the capabilities of personal workstations, mid-range computers, and mainframe computers; and that should foster the development of new products and services at an ever-increasing rate;

- systems should be easier to develop and maintain—via the use of new design and programming methods and tools (*object technology, component construction techniques, frameworks* and *patterns*)—and that should in turn foster the development of new business processes in a positive feedback cycle;

- systems should foster communications with customers— via new *user interfaces* at kiosks in malls and stores, via the *World Wide Web*, and via *client/server* technology that brings part of the system directly onto the end-user workstation, which will further their interest in new products and services; and

- systems should aid the introduction and delivery of new products and services—via a combination of all this technology in creative ways.

The continuing issue for IS and corporate management is how to foster the improvements attributable to new technology—and how to manage it. In the world of new information systems technology, you must:

- create systems based on a coherent architecture and architectural approach as the only way to build in the structural flexibility you will need in the future;
- analyze the implications of the new information technology supply chain and establish relationships with suppliers, vendors, and partners;
- establish "proof of technical architecture" as an on-going activity in the IS organization;
- recognize that system "requirements" are almost impossible to determine in the absence of a working system; that incremental and iterative development techniques are best suited to dealing with a changeable environment;
- increase the knowledge base of the organization using new technologies such as groupware and intelligent agents to improve knowledge management; and
- embrace the risk of new technology and find the strategies for minimizing its impact.

Being successful in this era of constant change means instituting processes that prepare your organization to move forward when all around you are running in random directions. I hope this book has given you some ideas on how to do that when the forward movement involves new information systems technology.

 Connections: **Connecting the Components**

There will always be new components of the new information systems technology. Our success in using them will be measured in the value that we can provide for our organizations. Realizing that value will require an understanding of how those components can be connected to form a value chain of systems and technology. And that is what this book has been about.

Bibliography

[Andersen 1992] Andersen, Espen, and Konsynski, Benn. "Brooklyn Union Gas: OOPS on Big Iron." Harvard Business School Case Study 9-192-144, June 1992.

[Badaracco 1991] Badaracco, Joseph L. *The Knowledge Link: How Firms Compete Through Strategic Alliances*. Harvard Business School Press (Boston), 1991.

[Band 1994] Band, William A. *Touchstones: Ten New Ideas Revolutionizing Business*. John Wiley and Sons (New York), 1994.

[Benjamin and Blunt 1992] Benjamin, R.I., and Blunt, J. "Critical Information Technology Issues: The Next Ten Years." in [Galliers 1994].

[Best 1990] Best, Larry. *Application Architecture*. John Wiley and Sons (New York), 1990.

[Best 1994] Best, Larry. "Organizational Readiness for Client/Server Systems." American Management Systems Focus Paper, September 1994.

[Beyer 1994] Beyer, D., Newell, M., and Hurst, I. "Grasping the Promise of Client-Server Computing." *The McKinsey Quarterly*, No. 3, 1994.

[Boehm 1988] Boehm, Barry W. "A Spiral Model of Software Development and Enhancement." *Computer Magazine*, May 1988.

[Bollier 1993] Bollier, David. *The Promise and Perils of Emerging Information Technologies*. The Aspen Institute (Washington, DC), 1993.

[Bouldin 1989] Bouldin, Barbara. *Agents of Change.* Yourdon Press/Prentice Hall, 1989.

[Bradley 1994] Bradley, A., "Client/Server Computing in the 1990s." Gartner Group Report CS:R-900-104, 1994.

[Brynjolfsson 1993] Brynjolfsson, E., and Hitt, L. "The Productivity Paradox of Information Technology." *Communications of the ACM*, December 1993.

[Capper 1994] Capper, N.P., Colgate, R.J., Hunter, J.C., and James, M.F. "The Impact of Object-oriented Technology on Software Quality: Three Case Histories." *IBM Systems Journal* 33, No.1.

[Cox 1992] Cox, Brad. "Superdistribution and Electronic Objects." *Journal of Object-oriented Programming*, June 1992.

[Cox 1995] Cox, Brad. "'No Silver Bullet' Reconsidered." *American Programmer*, November 1995.

[CWCSJ 1995] "Client/server Infrastructure Road Map." *Computerworld Client/Server Journal*, August 1995.

[Dec 1995] Dec, K. "Client/Server vs. Mainframe/Terminal Cost: The Data." Gartner Group Research Note CS:KA-810-299, 1995.

[Forman 1988] Forman, F., and Hess, M. "Form Precedes Function." *Computerworld*, September 5, 1988.

[Forrester 1995] "Vision: Can You Prove Your Value?" *The Forrester Report*, September 1995.

[Galliers 1994] Galliers, R.D., and Baker, B.S.H. Eds. *Strategic Information Management*. Butterworth-Heinemann Ltd. (Oxford), 1994.

[Gamma 1995] Gamma, Erich, Helm, Richard, Johnson, Ralph, and Vlissides, John. *Design Patterns: Elements of Reusable Object-Oriented Software.* Addison-Wesley (Reading, MA), 1995.

[Gause 1989] Gause, Donald, and Weinberg, Gerald. *Exploring Requirements: Quality Before Design*. Dorset House (New York), 1989.

[Goldberg and Rubin 1995] Goldberg, Adele, and Rubin, Kenneth S. *Succeeding With Objects.* Addison-Wesley (Reading, MA), 1995.

[Grady 1987] Grady, Robert B., and Caswell, Deborah L. *Software Metrics: Establishing a Company-Wide Program.* Prentice-Hall (Englewood Cliffs), 1987.

[Graham 1995] Graham, Ian. "Reuse: A Key to Successful Migration." *Object Magazine*, Vol. 5, No. 6.

[Grochow 1991] Grochow, Jerrold M. *SAA: Implementing IBM's Systems Application Architecture.* Yourdon Press/Prentice Hall (Englewood Cliffs), 1991.

[Grochow 1992] Grochow, Jerrold M. "Systems That Last 100 Years." *Information Week*, June 29, 1992.

[Grochow 1993] Grochow, Jerrold M. "Object's Bumpy Road." *CIO Magazine*, August 1993.

[Grochow 1994] Grochow, Jerrold M. "C/S Answer Lies in Objects." *Software Magazine*, March 1994.

[Grochow 1996] Grochow, Jerrold M. "The Myth of Open Systems." *PC Week Executive*, May 20, 1996.

[Hayes 1995] Hayes, Frank. "Bridging the Object Gap." *Information Week*, August 14, 1995.

[Hess 1993] Hess, Milton S. "What Did You Expect? A Task-Based Approach to Risk Management." *Best Practices Topic Papers*, American Management Systems (Fairfax, VA), 1993.

[Hess 1994] Hess, Milton S. "Writing Decision Papers." *Best Practices Topic Papers*, American Management Systems (Fairfax, VA), 1994.

[Hessinger 1994] Hessinger, Paul. "The Middleware Maze — Identifying a Taxonomy." *MiddlewareSpectra*, November 1994.

[Jones 1994a] Jones, Capers. *Assessment and Control of Software Risks.* Yourdon Press/Prentice Hall, 1994.

[Jones 1994b] Jones, Capers. "The Economics of Object-Oriented Software." *American Programmer*, October 1994.

[Jones 1995] Jones, Capers. "Risks of Software System Failure or Disaster." *American Programmer*, March 1995.

[Kaplan 1992] Kaplan, Robert S., and Norton, David P. "The Balanced Scorecard — Measures That Drive Performance." *Harvard Business Review*, January-February 1992.

[Keeney and Raiffa 1976] Keeney, Ralph L., and Raiffa, Howard. *Decisions with Multiple Objectives: Preferences and Value Tradeoffs*. John Wiley (New York), 1976.

[Knuth 1973] Knuth, Donald E. *The Art of Computer Programming*, Vol. 1: Fundamental Algorithms 2ed. Addison-Wesley (Reading, MA), 1973.

[Landauer 1995] Landauer, Thomas K. *The Trouble with Computers*. MIT Press (Cambridge), 1995.

[Lipton 1991] Lipton, James. *An Exaltation of Larks: The Ultimate Edition*, Viking Penguin (New York), 1991.

[Maes 1994] Maes, Pattie. "Agents That Reduce Work and Information Overload." *Communications of the ACM*, July 1994.

[Margolis 1990] Margolis, Nell. "High Tech Gets It There on Time." *Computerworld*, July 2, 1990.

[Martin 1992] Martin, James. "Reskilling the IT Professional," *Software Magazine*, October, 1992.

[Plewa and Pliskin 1995] Plewa, Jeffrey, and Pliskin, Steven. "Client/Server Everything." *CIO Magazine*, July 1995.

[Porter 1985-1] Porter, Michael E. *Competitive Advantage*. The Free Press (New York), 1985.

[Porter 1985-2] Porter, Michael E. "How Information Gives You Competitive Advantage." *Harvard Business Review*, July-August 1985.

[Ragland 1995] Ragland, Bryce. "Measure, Metric, or Indicator: What's the Difference?" *CrossTalk*, March 1995.

[Rogers 1983] Rogers, Everett M. *The Diffusion of Innovations, 3rd ed.* The Free Press (New York), 1983.

[Rosser 1993] Rosser, W. "Measuring IT Productivity at the Enterprise Level." Gartner Group Report IS:K-915-1020, 1993.

[Rubin 1995] Rubin, Howard, (Ed.). *IT Metrics Strategies*, February, 1995.

[Rubin 1995-2] Rubin, Howard. "Building an IT Management Flight Deck." *Computerworld (Leadership Series)*, October 16, 1995.

[Scherr 1987] Scherr, A.L., "Structures for Networks of Systems," *IBM Systems Journal*, 1987.

[Semich 1995] Semich, J. William. "The Rush to Objects Speeds Up." *Datamation*, June 1, 1995.

[Senge 1990] Senge, Peter M. *The Fifth Discipline*. Doubleday (New York), 1990.

[Soft 1995] "Survey of 100 Largest Software Vendors." *Software Magazine*, July, 1995.

[Somogyi 1987] Somogyi, E.K., and Galliers, R.D. "Information Technology in Business: From Data Processing to Strategic Information Systems." In [Galliers 1994].

[Statz 1995] Statz, Joyce, and Tennison, Susan. "Getting Started with Software Risk Management." *American Programmer*, March 1995.

[Strassman 1995] Strassman, Paul A. "Internet: A Way of Outsourcing Infomercenaries?" *American Programmer*, August. 1995.

[Taligent 1994] Taligent Corporation. "Building Object-Oriented Frameworks, A Taligent White Paper." World Wide Web URL http://www.taligent.com/building-oofw.html.

[Taligent 1995] Taligent Corporation. "CommonPoint Application System Data Sheet." World Wide Web URL http://www.taligent.com/commonpoint.html [no longer available].

[Taligent 1994-2] Taligent Corporation. "Leveraging Object-Oriented Frameworks, A Technology Primer from Taligent." World Wide Web URL http://www.taligent.com/Technology/WhitePapers/LeveragingFwks/LeveragingFrameworks.html

[Taylor 1990] Taylor, David A. *Object-Oriented Technology: A Manager's Guide.* Addison-Wesley (Reading MA), 1990.

[Terdiman 1996] Terdiman, R., and Schick, K. "The Great Business Crash of the Year 2000." Gartner Group Report ESP:TV-000-155, 1996.

[Tognazzini 1994] Tognazzini, Bruce. "The "Starfire" Video Prototype Project: A Case History*." Proceedings of CHI '94 Human Factors in Computing Systems*, ACM Press (New York), 1994.

[Tracz 1988] Tracz, W. *Software Reuse: Emerging Technology.* IEEE Computer Society Press (Los Alamitos, CA), 1988.

[Viljamaa 1995] Viljamaa, Panu. "The Patterns Business: Impressions from PLoP-94." *Software Engineering Notes*, January 1995.

[Walrad 1993] Walrad, C., and Moss, E. "Measurement: The Key to Application Development Quality." *IBM Systems Journal* 32, No. 3.

[Wang 1994] Wang, Charles B. *Techno Vision*. Mc-Graw Hill (New York), 1994.

[Womack 1990] Womack, J., Jones, D., and Roos, D. *The Machine That Changed the World: The Story of Lean Production*. Macmillan (New York), 1990.

[Yourdon 1989] Yourdon, Ed. "MCC," *American Programmer*, May 1989.

About the Author

Jerrold M. Grochow is a nationally noted consultant, speaker, and author on information systems technology. In his current position as Chief Technology Officer and Director of the Center for Advanced Technologies at American Management Systems, he consults with clients in government and industry on deploying the new information systems technologies for strategic business application. His previous book, *SAA: Implementing IBM's Systems Application Architecture*, was published by Yourdon Press in 1991.

Prior to beginning his career at AMS, Dr. Grochow worked at MIT's famed Project MAC (now the Laboratory for Computer Science) where he was a participant in the development of the Multics time-shared operating system, most widely known as the progenitor of UNIX. While working at MIT's Information Processing Services department in the early 1970s, he was involved in bringing MIT onto the ARPANet from which the Internet has grown.

Dr. Grochow received B.S., M.S., and Ph.D. degrees from MIT. He resides with his family in the Washington, DC, area.

Index

A

B

C

I

IBM 62, 138, 139, 157, 160, 166
incremental design 135
incremental development 198, 204, 267
information hiding 117
innovators 26
intelligent agents 220, 223, 267
International Function Point Users Group 236
International Standards Organization 65
Internet 53, 70, 138, 169, 258
Intranet 53, 70, 138
iterative design 135
iterative development 38, 198, 204, 211, 267

J

Java 72, 136, 137

K

Kiviat Plot 35

L

laggards 26
late majority 26
lean production 168, 170
legacy system 55, 61, 78
legal issues 257
life-cycle costs 226
logical architecture 93
Lotus 9, 182

M

mainframe systems 78
maintainability 89, 136
measurement 38, 231, 239
measurement dashboard 241
messages 118
metrics 231
Microsoft 68, 138, 166, 220
middleware 150, 190
migration strategy 55
Millennium Bug 91
modular systems 122
modularity 117
multi-dimensional databases 222
multiple inheritance 118
multi-tier system 51

N

NASDAQ 88
National Center for Supercomputer Applications 73
Netscape 72, 139
network architecture 83
network management 222
new information systems technology 1, 4
new technology, reasons for introducing 21
Novell 9

O

Object Management Group 186, 190
object request broker 68, 152
object technology 12, 113, 124, 189, 260, 266